SCHOOLING THE PREACHERS

The Development of Protestant Theological Education in the United States 1740–1875

James W. Fraser

UNIVERSITY
PRESS OF
AMERICA

Lanham • New York • London

Copyright © 1988 by

University Press of America,® Inc.

4720 Boston Way
Lanham, MD 20706

3 Henrietta Street
London WC2E 8LU England

Library of Congress Cataloging-in-Publication Data

Fraser, James W., 1944–
Schooling the preachers : the development of Protestant
theological education in the United States, 1740–1875 / James W. Fraser.
p. cm. Includes index.
1. Theology—Study and teaching—United States—History—18th
century. 2. Theology—Study and teaching—United States—
History—19th century. 3. Theological seminaries, Protestant—
United States—History—18th century. 4. Theological seminaries,
Protestant—United States—History—19th century. I. Title.
BV4030.F7   1988
207'.73—dc 19   88–20714 CIP
ISBN 0–8191–7160–3 (alk. paper)
ISBN 0–8191–7161–1 (pbk. : alk. paper)

To Nancy Richardson, Paul Deats, Bob Treese
and all those who struggle
for a more just and more humane
theological education in the twentieth century

Acknowledgments

The research on which this book is based began when the Lilly Endowment of Indianapolis, Indiana awarded a grant to Auburn Theological Seminary in New York City to support a study of the history of Protestant Theological Education in the United States. The "Auburn History project" team included Robert W. Lynn as director, and Virginia Brereton, Christa R. Klein, Glenn Miller, and Barbara Wheeler in addition to the author of this work. Many of the ideas included in this book were first developed in team discussions several years ago. In addition to the present volume, other members of the team will be publishing their portions of the final study during the next years. The author is grateful to the Seminary, the Endowment, and his colleagues in the history project for support, encouragement, and shared ideas.

The development of this volume also benefited from ongoing support from the Lilly Endowment and especially from Robert W. Lynn, Senior Vice President of the Endowment, without whose probing questions and constant encouragement at each stage this book would never have been completed. In addition, a number of other scholars contributed to the work of various chapters. Professor James Smylie of Union Theological Seminary, Richmond, Virginia, the editor of the Journal of Presbyterian History, contributed important questions and insisted on useful editorial changes in chapters one and three. I also want to thank Gerald W. Gillette, the associate editor of the Journal for his help in both the initial research and in the editing of this material. The impact of questions from Professor Timothy L. Smith of the Johns Hopkins University can be seen throughout Part II, and especially chapter six. Professor James E. Scanlon of Randolph-Macon College was very helpful in the development of chapter five, as were comments from Professor David Potts of Gettysburg College. Finally, Professor Earl Kent Brown of Boston University School of Theology read and offered helpful comments on chapter six. A number of people assisted with research along the way, including especially Ronald Huff and Christopher Frost.

Librarians and archivists throughout the country offered help and hospitality. Research included in this volume was conducted at the following locations: the Presbyterian Historical Society, Philadelphia, PA; the Historical Foundation of the Presbyterian Church, Montreat, NC; Oberlin College Archives, Oberlin, OH; the Methodist Board of Education, Nashville, TN; the Disciples of Christ Historical Society, Nashville, TN; the Walter Hines Page Library, Randolph-Macon College, Ashland, VA; the Olin Library, Wesleyan University, Middletown, CT; the Southern Baptist Historical Society, Nashville, TN; Andover Newton Theological School Library, Newton Centre, MA; Vanderbilt University Archives, Nashville, TN; the Georgia Department of Archives and History (the George Foster Pierce papers), Atlanta, GA; and the New England Methodist Historical Society at Boston University School of Theology.

The dedication to former colleagues from Boston University's School of Theology speaks of support which went far beyond the development of the current volume. My current colleagues at the University of Massachusetts/Boston have been generous with their time and understanding. I especially want to thank James Jennings and Sandra Kanter, Dean and Associate Dean respectively of the College of Public and Community Service, and Fuad Safwat, Dean of Graduate Studies for their encouragement. This book, and all of my recent research, has benefited from the support of the university's John W. McCormack Institute for Public Affairs, and the Institute's Director, Edmund Beard. Diane Dujon, the Assistant Director of Assessment at the College of Public and Community Service has carried more than her share of the load while this volume was prepared.

Finally, I want to thank the editors of various journals which had previously published some of this material in other forms for permission to republish it here. In earlier forms the following chapters appeared elsewhere:

Chapter one as "The Great Awakening and New Patterns of Presbyterian Theological Education," in the *Journal of Presbyterian History* 60:3 (Fall, 1982): 189-208.

Chapter two as "The Beginning of Theological Education at Andover" in the *Historical Journal of Massachusetts* XIII:2 (June, 1985): 101-116.

Chapter three as "Abolitionism, Activism, and New Models for Ministry," in *American Presbyterians: The Journal of Presbyterian History*, 66:2 (Summer, 1988).

Chapter six as "The Bishops, I Presume, Are Divided: Methodist Opposition to the Establishment of Vanderbilt University," *Southern Studies* XXIV:2 (Summer, 1985): 167-187.

Parts of Chapter four were previously presented as "Randolph-Macon, Wesleyan University— Methodist Schools: A Case Study in the Founding of Antebellum Colleges," to the Society for Historians of the Early American Republic Conference at Bentley College, Waltham, Massachusetts, July 23, 1983.

I also want to add a word of thanks to Rick Schwartz who did the typesetting and indexing and prepared the manuscript for publication.

Table of Contents

INTRODUCTION

The education of future ministers among Protestants in the United States changed significantly between 1740 and 1875. Indeed it was during these years that most of the institutional structure of contemporary theological education was built. This study of the schooling of the preachers focuses on six major changes or crises in these institutions. It is not a comprehensive study of all of the developments in the training of future clergy during these years. Rather this work focuses on a selection of examples which describe the general pattern of development in the institutions, formal and informal, devoted to the training of future ministers.

During these years the major institutional forms in which American Protestant clergy are trained took shape. Colleges certainly existed prior to these years, and many future ministers attended them. The first American colleges were begun in Massachusetts in 1636 and Virginia in 1693, but it was during the years after 1740 that colleges multiplied in number and spread throughout the new nation. The theological seminary did not exist at all among Protestants prior to 1808 but once begun at Andover, Massachusetts, this new institution spread rapidly. At the same time a variety of patterns of apprenticeship—reading divinity with a pastor or college professor, participating in a course of study outlined by the denomination while also serving as an apprentice preacher, or attending short term "preachers institutes"—arose and began to decline during these years. By 1875 the basic institutional pattern of Protestant theological education, four years of college followed by three years of theological seminary, was essentially in place. During the following century this pattern grew in terms of the numbers of future ministers who followed the option but not in the development of new structural models.

In looking at the six examples of the rise of various institutions for the training of future clergy presented here, a common pattern emerges. In each case change did not begin within the world of theological education itself. Instead a crisis developed over the understanding of the nature of the ministry or the nature of the Christian faith. Whether the crisis began over issues of the minister's work or more fundamental questions about the minister's faith, what had been a general consensus, within a denomination, or cluster of denominations, broke down. And with the crisis, a new institution or a new kind of institution was born. While the issues and the details differ significantly, the overall pattern remains quite clear. Changes in theological education are usually brought about by changes—by a crisis—in the understanding of the nature of the ministry which leads directly to shifts in the patterns of preparation for ministry.

The pattern can be seen quite clearly. Thus:

1) The Great Awakening of the 1740s led to fears about "the danger of an unconverted ministry," and the creation of new colleges to educate ministers for both the converted new light and orthodox old light Presbyterians.

2) The rise of Unitarianism brought a new demand among orthodox Congregationalists for orthodox ministers and a means of ensuring a steady supply of such ministers. To "check the prevalence of error," these Calvinists founded a new institution—and a new type of institution—Andover Theological Seminary.

3) Perfectionist Abolitionists, following Charles Finney demanded a minister—and a theological seminary—which was "not flattering the proud but pleading the cause of the poor;" and when none of the existent seminaries met their demands, they essentially refounded Oberlin College to meet the need.

4) As the nation grew, there were not enough college and seminary trained ministers to serve all of those in need, and many who were so trained seemed, to the new evangelicals, to be badly trained, so that they asked, "what in the world would have become of the masses of the people," if only college and seminary graduates were ordained. The result was a new, much more informal, pattern of theological education by apprenticeship among Methodists, Baptists, Cumberland Presbyterians and Disciples of Christ.

5) These same denominations soon discovered that the products of their apprenticeship systems did not meet the standards which they wanted nor were they able to compete with other

denominations. At the same time, they wanted to maintain their own identity independent from the older American denominations. As a result they argued, "nothing can save us but an able ministry and none can be had but through [college] education."

6) Finally, the demands for more professionally educated ministers came into a direct clash with the ideal of the Methodist circuit rider who was a 'man of the people' who depended only on the inspiration of the Holy Spirit. While some Methodists argued that, "a regular theological training, after the seminary pattern, will break down our itinerant system," the professional minister and the professional school came to these denominations as it had to others.

Whether it was Gilbert Tennent preaching about "the danger of an unconverted ministry," as he called his anti-revivalist opponents in 1740, or H. B. Stanton condemning Lane Seminary's trustees for conducting a school in which "the art of pleasing rather than saving men is the standard of excellence" because they rejected his abolitionism in 1835, or Alexander Campbell writing sarcastically of seminary students who "reads volumes of scholastic divinity," to be able to "deliver a very popular and orthodox sermon without any grace" in 1824, very similar issues emerged. In a wide variety of settings, and for a wide variety of reasons, reformers came to believe in a new understanding of the nature of the ministry. And once arriving at this point, they quickly also decided that the existing educational institutions were not capable of producing the new minister, and thus it was a logical step to starting a new institution.

New institutions were born not out of consensus and cooperation but out of turmoil and disagreement. Consensus might lead to cooperative discussions, but it seemed to take competition, hostility and the fear that the other side would make more progress before the work of founding a new institution—raising funds, hiring a faculty, attracting students—was actually done. But when a crisis did appear, when American Protestants split over significantly differing understandings of the nature of the ministry, then the next step was quite logical. One side—or in some cases both sides—founded new institutions to ensure the continuity of their own understanding of the nature of the ministry. While some of those institutions—especially the informal apprenticeship ones—have passed from the scene, many— including quite a few of the major colleges, universities, and theological seminaries of the northeast, south, and midwest—are with us today.

At some points in this history the nature of the ministry has been defined by a certain understanding of theological orthodoxy, at other times the test has been a certain role such as a revivalist or an abolitionist, and at other times as someone who met certain professional standards. But whatever the definition, a new definition has usually led its defenders to struggle to maintain it by finding new methods of educating the next generation of clergy so that they will fit the model.

All of these changes seem like quite logical developments. If the primary purpose of theological education is to train ministers for the churches, then the prime question in theological education must always be, "what is the nature of the ministry?" At times in the life of the church—and its educational institutions—there is a general consensus around the answer to this question. But at other times, that consensus dissolves in the face of internal or external forces. At such times, there is a crisis, and usually institutional change, as the world of theological education is brought to match the changed understanding of ministry. It is these crises which have led to the most significant institutional changes in the means of ministerial preparation among Protestants in the United States during these years.

PART I

THEOLOGICAL EDUCATION
FOR A CONVERTED MINISTRY

THE EVANGELICAL TRADITION
IN PRESBYTERIAN
AND CONGREGATIONAL BODIES

1

CHAPTER I
THE DANGER OF AN UNCONVERTED MINISTRY

THE GREAT AWAKENING AND NEW PATTERNS
OF PRESBYTERIAN THEOLOGICAL EDUCATION

In one of the famous sermons of the Great Awakening, "The Danger of an Unconverted Ministry" (1740), Gilbert Tennent called for a means of training pastors which would guarantee their loyalty to the cause of revivals: "The most likely method to stock the church with a faithful ministry, in the present situation of things, the public academies being so much corrupted and abused generally, is to encourage private schools, or seminaries of learning, which are under the care of skillful and experienced Christians..."[1] This rousing battle cry for the awakening forces was also a call for a new kind of minister and therefore, by implication, for a new form of theological education.

For Americans, an era of ferment—of religious awakening—has usually also been an era of change in the methods of theological education as new kinds of ministers are demanded by the churches to meet the new occasions produced by the awakening. In the nineteenth century both the three-year, post-college, theological seminary and some important new forms of apprenticeship were born out of the evangelical movements which covered the new nation after the War of 1812. But the Great Awakening of the 1730s and 1740s also had its own, perhaps less noted, reforms which change the forms of theological schooling of the day, and which continued to influence later developments for generations.

The Great Awakening transformed American religion and American institutions. Respected authorities were challenged, traditional patterns broken. New sects were born, free from the constraints of the old; while the existing denominations, especially the Presbyterians and Congregationalists, were bitterly divided between the pro- and anti-revival parties. Under the ministry of Jonathan Edwards and his predecessor, Solomon Stoddard, the town of Northampton, Massachusetts, and the Connecticut River valley experienced an extraordinary and surprising change in the early 1730s. Presbyterians including Jonathan Dickinson and Aaron Burr led similar developments in New York and New Jersey. Later, Gilbert Tennent stirred the revival in New Jersey and Pennsylvania while George Whitefield's tours from Maine to Georgia beginning in 1738 helped to spread the awakening through the colonies which would become the United States in what was probably the most uniting experience these disparate settlements had yet known.

The Awakening also split the Presbyterian church into two hostile bodies. Beginning with the exclusion of the Presbytery of New Brunswick in 1741 and culminating with the formation of the Synod of New York in 1745, the new side—or pro-revival—forces formed their own Presbyterian body, independent of the old side--or anti-revival--Synod of Philadelphia. Ironically, the church divided was much more creative in the development of theological education than the church united had been.[2]

A commitment to the best possible education for its ministers had been close to universal in the Presbyterian church, in Europe and in North America, from the earliest years. As early as 1710, in Pennsylvania, this commitment was tested:

> Upon information that David Evan, a lay person, had taken
> upon him publicly to teach or preach among the Welch in
> the Great Valley, Chester county, it was unanimously agreed
> that the said Evan had done very ill, and acted irregularly in
> thus invading the work of ministry, and was thereupon
> censured.[3]

In spite of a great shortage of ministers, the infant Presbytery of Philadelphia was not going to lower standards. Instead it ordered Evan to spend a year studying theology with three settled pastors before his examination for ordination. In fact, Evan spent four years in study, receiving a degree from Yale before his year of private theological study. He was finally ordained in 1714 and then returned to his preaching career.[4]

With the coming of the awakening in the 1730s, agreement about theological education became more difficult, not because Presbyterians differed on the need for quality education, but because they could not agree on what constituted a quality education for ministry. Even so, as late as 1739, Presbyterians were able to unite in a unanimous vote for "An overture for erecting a school or seminary of learning..."[5] While unanimity on that occasion may have been possible because of the absence of a few crucial individuals, the leaders of both factions were involved in the decision.

But votes and resolutions did not always lead to action. The old school leader Francis Alison was essentially right when he looked back to 1735 and wrote:

> That at my arrival here, there was not a College, nor even a good grammar school, in four Provinces, Maryland, Pennsylvania, Jersey, & New York...[6]

At the time of the division of the church in 1741, the only school serving primarily the Presbyterian church in North America in the training of ministers was William Tennent's school at Neshaminy, Pennsylvania, and that was clearly a school serving the new-side party, not the entire denomination. Other than studying with Tennent, Presbyterian ministers were either educated privately by reading with a more experienced minister, or by studying at a college in New England or Europe. Two decades later, however, at the time of the reunion of 1758, the Presbyterians would have numerous academies and two colleges devoted, at least in part, to the proper training of Presbyterian clergy.

It should not be so surprising that it took division to create institutions. Prior to Francis Alison's move to the Academy and College of Philadelphia in 1752 and Aaron Burr's move from his Newark, New Jersey parish to Princeton in 1756, there were no Presbyterian ministers engaged in full time teaching. Rather,

5

teaching was always something added on to the other responsibilities of a pastor. Resolutions were easy, but building institutions took time and money. And only the threat of another party's success seemed an adequate spur to that level of commitment.[7]

Certainly the threat worked. The period between 1741 and 1758 saw significant changes in Presbyterian theological education. The energies released by the awakening led to at least three important developments: the rise of the log college or academy, the founding of both a revival and an anti-revival college, and the expansion of an apprenticeship program of reading divinity, either after or in place of a college education.

Log Colleges and Academies

When Gilbert Tennent preached his controversial sermon in 1740, he brought to the occasion his own considerable experience with "private schools, or seminaries of learning, which are under the care of skillful and experienced Christians." His own education had begun in his father's home, well before that institution was transformed into one of the great educational institutions of colonial America. The "Log College" of Neshaminy, Pennsylvania, founded by William Tennent, would produce many of the leading revival clergy of the mid-eighteenth century.

The elder Tennent had gone to the University of Edinburgh before immigrating to America in 1706. While serving pastorates in New York and Pennsylvania, Tennent also developed a course of study for his sons, a program paralleling his own education in Scotland and Northern Ireland.[8] Sometime after settling in Neshaminy, Pennsylvania, in 1727, William Tennent opened the doors to others and in 1735 he purchased additional land and began using the log cabin attached to his home for the college.[9] Between 1735 and Tennent's retirement in 1742, the college was training two or three ministers a year.[10] Although it was a modest frame building, the work in the log cabin was significant, as George Whitefield said, in "bringing up gracious youths, and sending them out from time to time into the Lord's vineyard,"[11] and thereby filling a gap which had existed for want of a college between New Haven and Williamsburg.

Unfortunately no records were kept by the school, and the little we know is based on reminiscences of alumni and the writings of either friends or enemies. George Whitefield fondly noted in his journal:

> The place wherein the young Men study now is in contempt call'd *the College*...From this despised Place Seven or Eight worthy Ministers of Jesus have lately been sent forth; more are almost ready to be sent, and a Foundation is now laying for the Instruction of many others.[12]

Whitefield went on to note that, "The Devil will certainly rage against them..."[13] Whatever the Devil's action, the old side did rage about "Mr. W.T.'s great Slackness in educating Scholars under his Care, together with the plain Indications of the great Industry of his Sons to promote their Father's Scholars, tho' never so unqualified..."[14] More is known, however, about the later careers of some of the Log College's more illustrious graduates. Archibald Alexander has left a delightful sketch of some of the most famous Alumni of the Log College.[15] Among the lists were future college and academy presidents, and enough Presbyterian preachers to give the revival forces parity within the denomination. As late as 1758—sixteen years after the school had closed—ten of the ninety-six presbyterian ministers in the reunited Synod were graduates of this one school.[16]

The Log College was also important as the progenitor of many more schools, each of which would serve the revival cause in its own way. Among Tennent's graduates were Samuel Blair who established Fagg's Manor Academy and Samuel Finley who founded Nottingham Academy. And graduates of these academies went on to develop still more.[17]

One illustration of this pattern of academy-spawning-academy is the case of one of Tennent's early students, Samuel Blair. Like so many early Presbyterian ministers, Blair had been born in Ulster and emigrated to America with his family when he was ten. He studied with Tennent in the early 1730s, and was ordained in 1734. Upon moving to Faggs Manor, Pennsylvania, Blair led the parish through two important developments—

a revival which strengthened the life of the congregation, and the founding of an academy around 1740. In the school, Blair conducted classes in "the moral and physical sciences, as well as the languages, and theology."[18] While both future ministers and secular leaders studied with him, the school showed the influence of the revival. In addition to Robert Smith, who founded Pequea academy in Pennsylvania, Blair's alumni included Samuel Davies who would be President of Princeton college, and a number of Presbyterian ministers.[19] When Blair died in 1751, he was succeeded by his brother John Blair, who continued as both pastor and teacher until moving to Princeton as Professor of Divinity and acting President in 1757.[20]

The pattern at Fagg's Manor would be duplicated many times. Graduates of the school continued to move on and found additional schools. In all, Douglas Sloan has traced the development of 65 Presbyterian academies founded between the opening of the Log College and the end of the eighteenth century.[21] It was an institution well suited to its times.

The Tennents' success with their academy also galvanized the anti-revival forces of the Presbyterian church into action. One of the factors leading to the schism of 1741 was a resolution passed by the Synod of Philadelphia in 1739 which required an examination of "all such as had not obtained degrees in European or New England colleges, and give them certificates, if they were found qualified..."[22] On the surface the resolution seemed fair enough, but its actual consequences were that Yale and Irish-educated old-side candidates could enter the ministry without question, while every Tennent candidate endured the harassment of a hostile examination. Upholding standards, it seemed, also meant an attack on the school which most threatened the old-side position. Two years after the resolution—following prolonged debates over the ordination of some Tennent graduates—the Presbytery of New Brunswick was expelled from the Synod.[23] The old side and the new side were now two separate denominations.

Once the split had taken place however the old side moved quickly to plant their own school. As Archibald Alexander wrote later, "And now this school [the Log College] and all its friends and supporters were separated from the Synod; so that the need of a school where candidates might obtain at least the ground-work of a liberal education, was felt to be urgent..."[24] In spite of their 1739 resolution, the old-side did not want to depend on colleges in distant New England or Europe to train their clergy. Late in 1743 a committee of the Synod resolved on: "the necessity of using speedy endeavours to educate youth for supplying our vacancies."[25] Fortunately for the old side cause, Francis Alison, probably the most successful educator on the old side, had already established an academy of his own at his parish in New London, Pennsylvania in 1742. Born in Ireland in 1705, Alison studied at the University of Glasgow before coming to America in 1735. He had been pastor in New London since 1737, and would continue for many years to be a leading speaker and teacher for the old side.[26]

Rather than start a new school, the Synod in 1744 adopted Alison's as its own.[27] For the next eight years, Alison taught a steady stream of candidates, until he moved on to the Academy and later College of Philadelphia. After his departure, the school continued in its role, later moving to a more promising location in Newark, Delaware.[28]

Both sides continued to rely on the academy for decades. Even after the academies were replaced by or became feeders for the colleges on the Atlantic coast, new academies continued to provide new clergy for the expanding frontier. In short, as Douglas Sloan has written, "Much of the formal higher education available in the southern and western settlements of the eighteenth century took place in academies founded by Presbyterian ministers."[29]

The academies, significant as they were in the development of an American pattern of theological education, were also a temporary phenomenon. On the frontier the academies would continue for awhile as the only available schools for the teaching of minsters and other leaders. Yet in more settled areas the academy quietly changed its character. Either it became the nucleus for a college, or else a preparatory school for a nearby college. Either way, the college was the institution of the future, although that future might be very slow in coming.

At least four colleges—Princeton, Brown, Rutgers, and Dartmouth—normally trace their origins to the Great Awakening. Other colleges were also the result of that early eighteenth century upheaval. Kings College and the College of Philadelphia were aided by opponents of the awakening. Other colleges, especially on the southern and western frontiers, patterned themselves on those spawned by the awakening.[30]

Of course, colleges were not born from the awakening. Three important American colleges—Harvard, William & Mary, and Yale had been founded much earlier. From their earliest settlements, the English colonists wanted to continue their mother country's institutions in the face of the wilderness. Whether as a "city on a hill" for Puritan revolutionaries or as a retreat for trouble Loyalists, the colonists did not seek to reform college education but to reduplicate the best of what they knew from the old world in the microcosm of the new. With the awakening, however, the colleges began to declare their independence, form the old world and from each other.

William Tennent retired from his Neshaminy parish, closed his school in 1742, and died three years later. The new side leaders within the Presbyterian church were anxious to replace it.[31] According to Princeton tradition, it was a committee—four clergy and three laymen—who "first concocted the plan and foundation of the college."[32] A charter was issued in October of 1746 and classes were opened at Jonathan Dickinson's home in Elizabeth, New Jersey, the following year.

Princeton historians have long debated the proper founding date for the school—usually between the first and second charters of 1746 and 1748.[33] More significant, however, is the gradual evolution of the school from private study with one man to a college on its own campus. Well before 1746, Dickinson had taught candidates for the ministry who lived with him while pursuing their studies. William Sprague wrote correctly that, "it is probable that the office which he now formally assumed as President, occupied scarcely more of this time than he had previously devoted to the young men whose education he had undertaken to superintend."[34] When Dickinson died within the year, the college moved to the home of Aaron Burr in Newark, New Jersey, where the same pattern continued.[35] It was only in 1756, when Burr and seventy students moved from Newark to a new campus in Princeton, and Burr gave up his pastoral duties, that a full scale college can be said to exist. By 1756, however, the new side did have a college, modeled on the Yale which Dickinson and Burr remembered.

The College of New Jersey provided education closer to the heartland of Presbyterianism, and even more important, the opportunity to train clergy and laity in an atmosphere fully hospitable to the revivalistic movement. In varying forms, and with changing allegiance to the revival tradition, Princeton would dominate the training of Presbyterian clergy for many years to come.

While the transition of the College of New Jersey from private instruction to a full-fledged college was taking place, the enthusiasm for a college among some old side supporters was equally strong. In the resolution which had led to the adoption of the academy in New London, the old side leaders had noted that an academy was a temporary measure until more permanent institutions could be founded.[36] With Alison's move from New London to Philadelphia, the larger goal seemed within reach.

In December, 1751, the trustees of the Academy of Philadelphia elected Francis Alison to be its Rector, and he assumed the new duties early in the next year.[37] For the trustees of the Philadelphia school, which had opened in the spring of 1751 after several earlier attempts, Alison's old-side ties were much less significant than his educational ideas and ability as a teacher. Benjamin Franklin, one of the trustees, described the new teacher as, "a Dissenting minister, well skilled in those languages [Latin and Greek] and long practiced in teaching."[38] Clearly it was the skill and practice that mattered to the group which had founded a school not for ministerial training, but for

a proper Education of Youth, by forming their Manners, imbuing their tender Minds with Principles of Rectitude and Morality, instructing them in the dead and living Languages, particularly their Mother Tongue, and all usefull Branches of liberal Arts and Science.[39]

11

Whatever the trustees reasons for the choice, however, Alison's move was a stroke of very good luck for his old side colleagues, although some of them apparently were at first reluctant to part with him as head of their New London school.[40]

In 1754, Alison was joined by a second teacher, William Smith. Smith was Anglican, and for the next two decades the two would keep an uneasy eye on each other as they struggled to set the religious tone of the school.[41] Smith's arrival also made possible a second development. In 1755, after a proposal from Alison and Smith, "that it would probably be a Means of advancing the Reputation of the academy, if the Professors had a Power of conferring Degrees..."[42] the charter of the school was amended to make it the Academy and College of Philadelphia. Smith was to be Provost and Alison Vice-Provost while he continued to be Rector of the Academy. A year before the new side College of New Jersey had its own campus, the old side had a significant place within the new college in Philadelphia.

The College of Philadelphia would never be Presbyterian in the way that Princeton was. Even a reported proposal to establish ties between the college and the First Presbyterian Church of Philadelphia—where Alison was also associate pastor—was never completed.[43] The school had been founded by a group of prominent Philadelphians around Franklin, most of whom ranked the training of ministers relatively low on their concern for the college. For its first two decades its two major teachers would be a wary Episcopalian and a Presbyterian. After Alison's death in 1779 virtually all Presbyterian ties disappeared. But as long as he was there, he played a powerful role in the life of the school, and one part of that role was helping to train a generation of old side pastors who could receive both their classical training and instruction in divinity from this learned champion of their cause.

The role of the College of Philadelphia as an old side bastion was especially important during the first three years of its existence. From 1755 to 1758 Philadelphia and Princeton served two different denominations. After the reunion of 1758, Philadelphia's role became increasingly unclear. While not under the control of the Presbyterian Synod, Princeton was by its charter a Presbyterian school.[44] On the other hand, while

12

Alison and Smith might agree on academic policy, their theological struggles were acute. Eight years after the Presbyterian reunion Alison voiced his doubts about remaining since the Episcopal flavor at his own school had "inflamed our people with indignation against the College of Philad. Our students meet with hard measures from the ministers in ye favor of Jersey College..."[45] He wondered if in the future he would have many Presbyterian students.

By 1766 Alison's options were limited however. A number of old side people had proposed to the Princeton trustees that in the vacancy created by the death of President Samuel Finley they expand the faculty and "united all ye Presbyterians in the College of New Jersey," by electing Alison or one of his colleagues as the new President. The trustees, however, decided on a different method to unite all the Presbyterians around Princeton. Rather than turning to the old or new side, they had turned to Scotland and had "chosen one Wetherspoons, a Minister in Paisley in Scotland...[46] Alison was disappointed in the move, although he acknowledged that if the Scotsman should accept, "this would be a likely way to unite us."[47] In this judgment, Alison was right.

There were many reasons for Presbyterians to rally around Witherspoon and Princeton. A new generation was tired of the quarrels which had divided the denomination for so long. At the same time Witherspoon was a politician of considerable ability who knew how to rally a cause. By avoiding identifying overly with either faction, he was able to strengthen his own central position. Thus when Alison made the attempt in 1773 to raise funds for his old academy, now located in Newark, Delaware, Witherspoon moved to undercut this venture. He did not want competition, either theologically or academically, and he knew how to stop it.[48] Probably most important, however, by 1773, Alison was sixty-eight years old and still quarreling with that "absurd thing, a vote of ye Majority..." of the Synod.[49] But the sense of party was ebbing. The estrangements of the awakening seemed old. By his energy and his central position, Witherspoon was in the position to inspire and rally his church, and his college became one of the unifying points.

The enthusiasm for colleges spawned by the awakening also

continued to flourish in the south and west long after the awakening itself had run its course. In Virginia, Hanover Presbytery supported two academies both of which would eventually become colleges. In 1776 in western Virginia, the Presbytery adopted a school which had been founded in 1749, Augusta Academy, and in a burst of revolutionary enthusiasm renamed it Liberty Hall. Under its new principal, William Graham, the schools announced a program "where all the most important branches of learning, necessary to prepare young gentlemen for the study of Law, Physic and Theology may be taught to good advantage..."[50] Many years later the school would develop into Washington and Lee University.

On the other side of the state, a recent Princeton graduate and future Princeton president, Samuel Stanhope Smith opened the second academy with the Presbytery's blessing in Augusta in 1774.[51] The school advertised:

> In the Academy which Mr. Smith has the prospect of conducting in Pr: Edward County, according to the request and appointment of the Presbytery of Hanover, if he meets with the encouragement he expects; shall be taught the Greek and Latin languages to their greatest extent; and all the Sciences which are usually studied, at any College, or Academy on the Continent.[52]

Smith received the encouragement he sought. Two years later the school reopened as Hampden-Sydney College, to serve in Virginia as Princeton did in the North.[53]

Further south in North Carolina, Princeton graduates worked with Scotch-Irish immigrants to establish a number of academies, including the famous Clio's Nursery in Iredell County where "instruction was given which was regarded as sufficient for receiving a license as a minister in the Presbyterian Church." Once the academy was in operation, the next logical step was the establishment of a college. And so the Presbyterians opened Davidson College to extend their system of education, both classical and theological.[54]

On the western frontier, John McMillan helped to found such disparate institutions as Cannonsburg Academy and Washington Academy, Jefferson College, and Western Theological Seminary. By the 1780s, there were flourishing classical academies in McMillan's part of western Pennsylvania, and by the first decade of the new century a four-year college with a professor of divinity had appeared on the scene.[55]

The awakening produced a host of new institutions and significantly modified those already in existence. Yet there is an irony in the development of these schools, for the founding of colleges also exacted a price. While William Tennent could open his academy to prepare a few students for the revival ministry as he believed it should be exercised, those seeking a college charter and endowment for Princeton or for Philadelphia, had to find a broader base. They opened the school to all denominations and to students preparing for the several professions. In time, without the founders necessarily realizing what was happening, this broader scope also moderated the power of their initial focus. In effect, as Lawrence Cremin has noted, "The very academies and colleges that were established to perpetuate the awakenings ended up taming them...[56] It would not be the last time such a story would be told.

Reading Divinity

While the awakening was significant in the spread of new colleges, its anti-establishment nature also caused many to distrust colleges, at least as the final stage of preparation for ministry. And so, after many of the "awakened" finished college (and for some even prior to finishing) they decided to spend anywhere from a few months to a year or more in the home of one of the revival preachers studying theology, and learning the techniques of revival preaching, and the practical details of parish life.[57]

Such an approach to the training of future ministers was not new. From the first days of Harvard, some of its graduates chose to spend the next three years as residents on campus or in the home of a friendly pastor, studying before returning to the college for their masters examinations.[58] Among Presbyterians, reading divinity was also popular long before the awakening. Jonathan Dickinson spent two years in private study after he graduated from Yale in 1706 before he was licensed to preach.[59] Others followed the same course.

With the advent of the awakening, however, reading divinity took on a new importance in the preparation of Presbyterian ministers. In the more settled areas, candidates who did attend college could still spend another year or two after college with a pastor especially close to their own position. Thus when John McMillan graduated from Princeton in 1772, although he had studied with a sympathetic John Witherspoon, he returned home to Pequea Academy in Lancaster County, Pennsylvania, to spend another year studying theology with the more clearly pro-revivalist Robert Smith.[60]

A more extreme example is the case of John Ewing. A graduate and sometime tutor at Francis Alison's New London academy, Ewing was clearly part of the old side. Yet, when he was ready for College, the transformation at Philadelphia had not yet happened, and he attended the College of New Jersey, graduating in 1774. He continued for a time as a tutor with President Burr, but then rejoined his old mentor, Francis Alison, for a period of reading divinity in his own tradition.[61] It was a theological education with more theological variety than most, but the movement from college to friendly tutor in theology was typical, especially at a time when loyalty to a particular party was especially important in a contentious Presbyterian church.

An alternative method of reading divinity was for the candidate to remain at college after graduation to study with the president. Apparently this was what Ewing did with Burr for a brief time, and many who found themselves more sympathetic to the college's theology followed the pattern. At Philadelphia this was also clearly part of Vice-Provost Alison's role.[62] At many European colleges, and at Harvard, a professorship in Divinity was also established. For the most part, the professor of divinity was simply an auxiliary to the president and assisted by supervising the resident graduates in their reading of divinity while also instructing undergraduates.[63]

Princeton established a professorship of Divinity in 1767, just after the death of President Samuel Finley, and elected John Blair, the head of Fagg's Manor academy, as the professor.[64] Blair held the position, and also served the college as

Vice-President and acting President, until the newly elected John Witherspoon arrived in 1768. Soon after Witherspoon's arrival, however, Blair resigned all of his offices.[65] The official reason given by Blair was that his role, "may devolve upon the President, and thereby the expense of my salary be saved..."[66] Cost was a significant factor for a small, struggling, institution. But equally important, John Witherspoon meant to be his own theologian. He would set the tone, and the students would study with him. For many Presbyterian ministers in the next two generations, study with Witherspoon would indeed be the pattern of their theological education.[67]

While the colleges at Princeton and Philadelphia both began to offer opportunities for a theological education in the middle of the eighteenth century, not all prospective ministers chose that route. John Rodgers, who would play a significant role as a New York City pastor, attended two academies, and then transferred to Fagg's Manor where he finished his classical work and studied theology with Samuel Blair. Finally, he continued his theological education in Philadelphia with Gilbert Tennent.[68] While becoming more available, college was far from the only route to ministry. A classical education, followed by study in theology was required for ordination, and there were many ways to accomplish that.

The alternatives to college study were especially important on the sparsely settled regions of western Virginia, the Carolinas, and what would become Tennessee. In these regions, Presbyterian churches often found it necessary to educate their own candidates rather than risk the expense and danger of sending them north or east for college. Of course, many college-trained pastors had come with the other settlers. But there were never enough of these college educated ministers; a generation of native clergy had to be trained. The result was a fairly carefully organized program of reading divinity, administered by the Presbyteries which would also eventually examine the candidate for ordination. Thus the *Memoir of the Rev. Samuel Davies* reported on his work in Virginia prior to 1759 that he,

doubtless gave an impulse to the minds of his co-presbyters, and of the students in Divinity raised up under the care of

17

Hanover Presbytery. In the oldest records of this body, we read of candidates for the ministry being examined on "Latin, Greek, and Hebrew; on Ontology, Pneumatics, and Astronomy," as well as on the various branches of Theological learning.[69]

These programs also continued long after the awakening had run its course, and after several coastal colleges had become available to Presbyterians.

In one example, the Presbytery of Concord, North Carolina, at its meeting of March 30, 1797, included in its minutes the notice that "The Presbytery was informed by one of their members that Mr. McElheney had been reading Divinity under his care the last term...[70]

McElheney's curriculum in reading divinity was not haphazard. At a previous meeting the Presbytery had adopted the curriculum they expected of a candidate for this form of theological training:

1. No candidate for the ministry shall be received under the care of this Presbytery until he shall have stood satisfactory examination on the whole series of Languages & Sciences usual in such cases except he produce a Diploma from a chartered College or University.

2. At each succeeding Stated Session for the space of two years, except ordered otherwise by the Presbytery, each candidate shall stand an examination on the following subjects: At the first session on the subjects contained in the first eight chapters of the Confession of Faith & on the History of the Christian Church during the five first centuries. At the second and third sessions he shall be examined on the same number of the next succeeding chapters & centuries & at the fourth session on the subjects contained in the last nine chapters of the Confession & on the History of the Church during the 17 & 18th centuries.

3. Besides the above each candidate shall deliver on subjects previously assigned him a sermon and a Latin Exegesis at the first session after entrance; at the second Session a Sermon and an English Exegesis; at the third a Sermon & Exhortation; at the fourth a Popular Lecture & sermon—both to be delivered *memoriter*; and at said Session he shall stand a general examination on English Grammar, Criticism & the Rules of Oratory, Chronology & the government of the Church.[71]

Further minutes of the Presbytery indicate that Mr. McElheney was examined in some detail on his work in reading divinity and then approved for ordination.

Not every Presbytery had a curriculum as clearly outlined as Concord's, but most did have provisions for reading divinity on the part of their candidates. For instance, Abingdon Presbytery in Virginia resolved that "the candidate under our care be called upon to inform presbytery with whom they wish to pursue their studies."[72] That same group also attempted to build a theological library for their students:

> On motion, it was agreed to employ the Rev. Johnney Doak
> to solicit donations in books in Philadelphia and elsewhere,
> suitable for students in divinity and to have them forwarded,
> as soon as convenient, to some place within the bounds of
> the presbytery, for the use of students under their care.[73]

Candidates studying with preachers were expected to appear regularly to be tested on their progress and to appear for a rigorous final examination in preaching, exegesis, and doctrine.[74]

There are, of course, limits to what can be known about these programs. How much flexibility did a candidate have? How rigorously were standards applied? The records raise as many fascinating questions as they answer. Nevertheless, the existence of this curriculum in the midst of handwritten Presbytery minutes remains a symbol of the attempt of people struggling on a new frontier to maintain a high level of theological standards for their successors in the ministry, even when colleges could not be supported.

The program of study in divinity which flourished on the frontier through the turn of the nineteenth century, combined with the numbers of institutional developments among Presbyterians educators in the two decades after the schism of 1741 is impressive. But these programs were made easier by the fact that while Presbyterians might quarrel furiously about theological issues or the means of salvation, and while they might regularly accuse each other of lowering the standards of ministerial education, there was a surprisingly wide range of agreement as just what, in fact, did constitute a proper theological education. The European curriculum of classical and theological studies, imported primarily by way of Scotland and Northern Ireland, formed the basis of all the theological curricula of the eighteenth century.

When Francis Alison charged the Log College with "Slackness in educating Scholars..."[75] the Tennents did not respond with any challenge to the importance of scholarship, but only that Alison's judgments were incorrect. In return when the New London Academy was advertised as a place "where the Language, philosophy, and divinity should be taught"[76] the newside did not charge the school with studying the wrong things, but only of studying with a cold heart. While the institutional forms might vary greatly, there was enough of a consensus about the content of the training so that when the North Carolina Presbytery ordered candidates to know "the whole series of Languages & Sciences usual in such cases," everyone knew what was involved.

The Latin and Greek classics were the base. Further study in biblical languages and the major theologians of the Reformation were the theological superstructure. In the awakening of the eighteenth century, as they would in the nineteenth century, calls for a new spirit in the churches or the ministry did not become calls for a new content to the theological curriculum, but only for a new spirit—and often a new institutional basis—for the instruction.[77]

The question naturally arises why one party or the other did not call for a significant change in the content of Presbyterian theological education as a result of the issues raised by the awakening, especially in regard to the heavy emphasis on the Latin and Greek classics. Such challenges would be the heart of the debates about theological education after 1800. The most simple answer is that it just had not occurred to anyone. Presbyterian patterns of theological education had been imported from Britain during the preceding century. But theological education, either in England or Scotland, was not a separate branch of learning; rather it constituted a basic part of the education necessary for a "learned gentleman" whether that gentleman was to go on to a career in the pulpit or another sphere of public leadership.

A brief look at the earliest colonial colleges makes this point quite vividly. In the royal charter for the College of William and Mary, issued in 1693, it was stated that the goal was to, "...establish a certain place of universal study, or perpetual College of Divinity, Philosophy, Languages, and other good Arts and Sciences..."[78] Divinity was not to be separated from the other "good Arts and Sciences". Similarly, Harvard's historian Samuel Eliot Morrison has written of his institution, "Their Arts curriculum was almost entirely taken over from classical antiquity...There was no special vocational training for the priesthood..."[79]

The general agreement seems to have been clear. The general education necessary for all colonial leaders was the same. Colleges remained the ideal place for this basic education to take place. But if there were no colleges nearby, Presbytery examining committees would still conduct their examinations to make sure that the study took place, whether through private work, reading with a respected pastor, or schooling at an academy. The leaders of either party in the awakening might lay increased emphasis on the theological superstructure. But to remove the classical base was to remove ministers from the ranks of society's educated elite. Neither pro- nor anti-revivalist was ready for that move.

Because of the fundamental agreement on the content of theological education, the forms were also much less significant, except as they represented rallying points for various factions. By 1758 it was certainly possible for a ministerial candidate to go from academy to college to a year of reading divinity. Some candidates did just that. But many more did not. The important thing was to receive all the elements of a proper education.

It was this lack of concern for a progression from one institution to another that made it possible for John Ewing to study first at the College of New Jersey and then with Alison at the College of Philadelphia, while John Rodgers attended three academies and no college.[80] Another future Presbyterian minister, Eliezer Whittlesey, began his theological studies with Aaron Burr in 1741-42 before the College of New Jersey was founded. Apparently Whittlesey did not do well and dropped out for a time. Later he returned to classical study with Samuel Finley in

West Nottingham, Maryland, and then in 1747 returned to study with Dickinson and then with Burr again at the newly founded college.[81] yet another future pastor, David Rice, was influenced in his decision to enter the ministry by Samuel Davies in Virginia and began his preparation at an academy in his native state. When Davies was elected President of the College of New Jersey in 1759, however, Rice took this as an excellent opportunity to rejoin his old mentor, and so accompanied him north. He was admitted to the junior class of the college because of his previous work, graduated in 1761, and then returned for further theological study with his academy teacher, John Todd.[82] Such flexibility in the use of institutions for the larger goal of proper education is unimaginable in the twentieth century. In the eighteenth century, however, such moves were thoroughly acceptable means of accomplishing the goal.

Indeed, the standards for a proper education were much more clearly set than the meaning of a particular institutional name. The distinction between an academy and a college was always vague prior to the revolution.[83] David Caldwell's Newbern Academy in North Carolina was described as "an Academy, a College, and a Theological Seminary."[84] While there is exaggeration in the statement, the school did serve some future ministers as a preparatory school, while others received their complete theological education there.[85] Even Francis Alison, certainly not one to relax educational standards, argued as late as 1773 that the Newark, Delaware Academy provided an adequate theological education for ministry in comparison to "ye Colleges in this City, & in Princeton."[86] By the 1770s the new institutions had arrived on the stage of American Presbyterianism. But a different generation would have to bring order to the pattern.

The Revolutionary War stopped the development of schools in nearly all their forms. All of the colonial colleges were disrupted at one time or another. Many who might have spent time reading divinity joined the army. The Great Awakening of the 1740s had set off many waves of reform in theological education across the spectrum of American Protestants. In the succeeding twenty years new adjustments were made. But by the 1770s the energy of the awakening had dissipated. Only in a new century

22

and a new era of religious enthusiasm would the ideas, time, and money necessary for significant reform of theological education again be available. The time was ripe for a second Great Awakening in theological education as in religion at large.

FOOTNOTES

[1] Gilbert Tennent, "The Danger of an Unconverted Ministry, Considered in a Sermon on Mark: 6:34" (2nd., Boston: Rogers and Fowle, 1742), p. 12.

[2] For a description of the Presbyterian division, see: Maurice W. Armstrong, Lefferts A. Loetscher, and Charles A. Anderson, *The Presbyterian Enterprise: Sources of American Presbyterian History* (Philadelphia: The Westminster Press, 1956), pp. 33ff.

[3] *Records of the Presbyterian Church*, 1710, p. 17, cited in Armstrong, p. 19.

[4] Thomas Clinton Pears, Jr., "Colonial Education Among Presbyterians," *The Journal of the Presbyterian Historical Society* XXX (June & September, 1952): 115-126 & 165-174, pp. 119-120.

[5] John MacLean, *History of the College of New Jersey*, 2 Vols. (Philadelphia: J.B. Lippincott & Co., 1877), I: p. 26.

[6] Francis Alison to Ezra Stiles, Philadelphia, December 12, 1767, photocopy, Presbyterian Historical Society, Philadelphia, Pennsylvania.

[7] Thomas Pears wrote of the Log College, "The unfortunate thing about it all is, that this School should have identified itself so completely with what was after all *a party* in the Church." (Pears, p. 126). from the perspective of a united denomination it may have been unfortunate, but from the perspective of change and development in theological education, it was probably the only way.

[8] For a useful study of the Scottish and Irish influence on the American Presbyterian academies, see Douglas Sloan, *The Scottish Enlightenment and the American College Ideal* (New York: Teachers College Press, 1971), pp. 38-47.

[9] Pears, pp. 121-122.

[10] Pears, pp. 121-122.

[11] George Whitefield, *Journal*, quoted in A. Alexander, *Biographical Sketches of the Founder and Principal Alumni of the Log College* (Philadelphia: Presbyterian Board of Publication, 1851), p. 19.

[12] ibid.

[13] ibid.

[14] *An Examination and Refutation of Mr. Gilbert Tennent's Remarks on the Protestation*, & c. (Philadelphia: Printed by B. Franklin, 1742) cited in Thomas C. Pears and Guy S. Klett, comps., "A Documentary History of William Tennent and the Log College," (Mimeographed manuscript; Philadelphia: Presbyterian

Historical Society, 1940), p. 161.

[15] Alexander, cited above.

[16] Leonard J. Trinterud, *The Forming of an American Tradition* (Philadelphia: The Westminster Press, 1949), p. 152.

[17] Sloan, pp. 55-56. Academies on the frontier were not infrequently called "Log Colleges." See Samuel Tyndale Wilson, *A Century of Maryville College, 1819-1919: A Story of Altruism* (Maryville, Tennessee: Directors of Maryville College, 1916), pp. 21-22 for a discussion of Isaac Anderson's log college, the predecessor of Maryville College.

[18] J.D. Edmiston Turner, "Reverend Samuel Blair, 1712-1751," *The Journal of the Presbyterian Historical Society* XXIX (December, 1951): p. 232.

[19] William B. Sprague, "An Introductory Memoir of President Davies," in *Sermons by the Rev. Samuel Davies, A.M.* 3 Vols. (Philadelphia: Presbyterian Board of Publication, 18) I, p. 12.

[20] Turner, pp. 229 & 232; MacLean, p. 292.

[21] Sloan, p. 38.

[22] Minutes, Presbyterian Board of Education, p. 4, quoted in Trinterud, pp. 73-74.

[23] Armstrong, p. 34ff.; and William B. Sprague, *Annals of the American Pulpit*, Vol. III: *The Presbyterians* (New York: Robert Carter & Brothers, 1858), "Introduction," p. xiii.

[24] Alexander, pp. 86-87.

[25] Armstrong, p. 54.

[26] Thomas Harrison Montgomery, *A History of the University of Pennsylvania from its Foundations to A.D. 1770* (Philadelphia: George W. Jacobs & Co., 1900), p. 163. Montgomery's study provides an excellent history of the early years of the university.

[27] ibid.; see also Francis Alison to Ezra Stiles, Philadelphia, May 7, 1768, photocopy, Presbyterian Historical Society, Philadelphia, Pennsylvania.

[28] Francis Alison to Ezra Stiles, Philadelphia, October 22, 1773; Montgomery, pp. 163-164.

[29] Sloan, p. 38.

[30] For a useful overview of the development of colonial colleges, see Frederick Rudolph, *The American College and University* (New York, 1962).

[31] MacLean, pp. 31-32. MacLean questions how directly the transition from Neshaminy to Princeton was. In any case, by 1744 the new side was without a school and its leaders wanted one.

[32] Jonathan Dickinson MSS. Letter of march 3, 1747, Princeton University Library, Princeton, N.J., quoted in Thomas Jefferson Wertenbaker, *Princeton, 1746-1896* (Princeton: Princeton University Press, 1946), p. 15.

[33] MacLean, pp. 114-127.

[34] Sprague, *Annals*, III, p. 16.

[35] MacLean, p. 127.

[36] Armstrong, p. 54.

37 Montgomery, p. 162.

38 Benjamin Franklin to Rev. Dr. Johnson, July 2, 1752, cited in Montgomery, pp. 162-63.

39 "Constitution of the Publick Academy in the City of Philadelphia," Montgomery, p. 46.

40 Sprague, *Annals*, III, p. 74.

41 Sloan, pp. 82-83.

42 Montgomery, p. 164.

43 Edward Potts Cheyney, *History of the University of Pennsylvania, 1740-1940*. (Philadelphia: University of Pennsylvania Press, 1940), p. 40.

44 MacLean, pp. 63-64.

45 Francis Alison to Ezra Stiles, Philadelphia, December 4, 1776.

46 ibid.

47 ibid.

48 Francis Alison to Ezra Stiles, Philadelphia, October 22, 1773; Sloan, pp. 81-82 & 114.

49 Alison to Stiles, October 22, 1773.

50 Ernest Trice Thompson, *Presbyterians in the South*, Vol. I, *1607-1861* (Richmond, Virginia: John Knox Press, 1963) pp. 80-81.

51 Herbert Clarence Bradshaw, *History of Hampden-Sydney College* Vol. I. *From the Beginning to the Year 1856* (Privately Printed, 1976) pp. 11-13.

52 Bradshaw, p. 14.

53 Bradshaw, p. 14; and Thompson, pp. 81-82.

54 Donald Robert Come, "The Influence of Princeton on Higher Education in the South Before 1825," *The William and Mary Quarterly* 2, (Third Series, October 1945), pp. 378-381.

55 Dwight Raymond Guthrid, John McMillan: *The Apostle of Presbyterianism in the West, 1752-1833* (Pittsburgh: University of Pittsburgh Press, 1952), pp. 70-81.

56 Lawrence A. Cremin, *American Education: The Colonial Experience 1607-1783* (New York: Harper & Row, 1970), p. 332.

57 For a useful study of reading programs in New England see Mary Latimer Gambrell, *Ministerial Training in Eighteenth Century New England* (New York: Columbia University Press, 1937); and William Tolbert Vandever, Jr., "An Educational History of the English and American Baptists in the Seventeenth and Eighteenth Centuries," (Ph.D. dissertation, University of Pennsylvania, 1974), p. 306.

58 Samuel Eliot Morison, *Harvard College in the Seventeenth Century* 2 Vols. (Cambridge: Harvard University Press, 1936), I: 272-280.

59 Sprague, *Annals*, III, p. 14.

60 James D. Moffat, *Pioneer Educators in Washington County, Pa.* (Nashville, Tennessee: Barbee & Smith, 1896), p. 9.

61 Sprague, *Annals*, III, p. 217.

[62] Francis Alison to Ezra Stiles, December 4, 1766; see also Cheyney, p. 40.

[63] Gambrell, p. 93.

[64] Sprague, *Annals*, III, pp. 117-118.

[65] Samuel J. Baird, *A History of the Early Policy of the Presbyterian Church in the Training of Her Ministry; and of the First Years of The Board of Education* (Philadelphia: Board of Education of the Presbyterian Church, 1865), pp. 12-14.

[66] John Blair to Gentlemen, April 6, 1769, cited in MacLean, p. 305.

[67] Sloan, pp. 113-115.

[68] Sprague, *Annals*, III, pp. 154-155.

[69] *Memoir of the Rev. Samuel Davies* (Boston: Massachusetts Sabbath School Society, 1832), p. 84.

[70] Montreat, North Carolina, Historical Foundation of the Presbyterian Church in the United States, Records of Concord Presbytery (formed October 2, 1745 by the Synod of the Carolinas) handwritten minutes, vol. 1:30. The author wishes to thank the Historical Foundation for their special helpfulness in the research which led to this paper.

[71] Concord Presbytery, pp. 19-21., October 27, 1796.

[72] Montreat, North Carolina, Historical Foundation of the Presbyterian Church in the United States, Minutes of the Abingdon Presbytery, handwritten minutes, vol. 1:45.

[73] Abingdon Presbytery, p. 44.

[74] Concord Presbytery, pp. 7-8, 29-30; Abingdon Presbytery, p. 49.

[75] *An Examination and Refutation*, in Pears & Klett, compilers, p. 161.

[76] Pears, "Colonial Education," p. 169.

[77] See Sloan, p. 59ff.

[78] *The History of the College of William and Mary, from its Foundation, 1693 to 1870* (Baltimore: John Murphy & Co., 1870), p. 3.

[79] Samuel Eliot Morison, *The Founding of Harvard College* (Cambridge: Harvard University Press, 1935), pp. 7-8.

[80] See Sprague, *Annals*, III, pp. 154-155; 216-217.

[81] James McLachlan, *Princetonians—1748-1768—A Biographical Dictionary* (Princeton: Princeton University Press, 1976) p. 23.

[82] Sprague, *Annals*, III, p. 246.

[83] Sloan, p. 59ff.

[84] E.W. Caruthers, *A Sketch of the Life and Character of the Rev. David Caldwell, D.D.* (Greensborough, N.C.: Printed by Swain and Sherwood, 1842), p. 37.

[85] ibid., pp. 30-31.

[86] Francis Alison to Ezra Stiles, October 22, 1773.

Chapter II

SOMETHING MUST BE DONE TO CHECK
THE PREVALENCE OF ERROR

THE FOUNDING OF ANDOVER THEOLOGICAL SEMINARY
FOR THE EDUCATION OF ORTHODOX, TRINITARIAN
MINISTERS IN NEW ENGLAND

Edward Door Griffin, later to be Andover Seminary's first professor of sacred rhetoric, remembered his youth in western Connecticut: "I saw a continued succession of heavenly sprinklings...until, in 1799, I could stand at my door in New Hartford, Litchfield County, and number fifty or sixty contiguous congregations laid down in one field of divine wonders."[1] Later Barton W. Stone, at the time pastor of the Presbyterian Church in Cane Ridge, Bourbon County, Kentucky, described the camp meeting of 1801 which would make his village forever famous in the annals of American revivalism: "Many things transpired there, which were so much like miracles, that if they were not, they had the same effects as miracles on infidels and unbelievers..."[2] These "heavenly sprinklings" and "miracles" were the harbingers of what became known throughout the new nation as the Second Great Awakening.

Many New England parishes and pastors, especially among those who considered themselves heirs of the Great Awakening of the 1730s and 40s, began to experience new revivals of religious concern and energy during the 1790s. A revival at Yale College under its influential president, Timothy Dwight, in 1801 brought further attention to the movement, while also helping to convert many who became the preachers of the awakening as it

29

continued to spread.

Soon revivals became expected features of much of New England congregational life, and a church went too long without one was either to be pities or censured. But there was more to the revival movement than just preaching and soul saving. Dwight and his successors had an agenda for New England and America, and the awakening was the vehicle for accomplishing it. In Dwight's estimate, the Revolutionary generation had moved away from the faith of the Puritans to an Enlightenment rationalism. The genteel deism of a majority of the Yale student body when he arrived in 1797 was simply proof of the problem, while the results of this deism in revolutionary France, coupled with his perceptions of the barbarism of the American frontier, gave him much to fear.[3] And so the awakening was the method to return the nation to its true faith.[4]

In their quest to transform the land, and confound those who opposed them—especially the anti-Calvinist Unitarians— the evangelicals like Dwight relied most of all on education. In those early decades these church leaders came to trust a newly-evident cluster of educational institutions: for the masses, the church with its college-trained pastor and the public school and Sunday school; and for the leaders, the college and a new institution—the theological seminary.[5]

Beginning with the founding of Andover Theological Seminary in 1808, the three-year seminary, an institution independent of colleges and designed for the post-collegiate training of clergy, became a characteristic of the evangelical crusade wherever its influence and energy was felt. In New England, across New York, and into the Mississippi Valley, theological seminaries were founded, modeled to a degree on their predecessor at Andover, to carry on the work of training new leaders for the crusade. The seminary was even adopted by others who did not share the evangelicals' enthusiasm—Unitarian Harvard itself established a Divinity School in 1815—but the institution had begun with the revivalists. The new form of schooling developed first an Andover, Massachusetts, has served many needs in the almost two centuries since its beginning. Its roots, however, are in a very specific set of historic needs and opportunities. At that point a new institutional model was born, one significant enough to deserve more attention that it has received to date.

Leonard Woods, destined to be a major speaker for their cause, described the mood among Massachusetts' evangelicals in 1806: "This state of things in Boston and Cambridge caused deep solicitude among Orthodox ministers and Christians, and led to a general feeling that something must be done to check the prevalence of error."[6] The first years of the nineteenth century were not easy ones for those who supported the revivals associated with the Second Great Awakening in New England. In the fall of 1800 their arch-enemy, the deist Thomas Jefferson, was elected President of the new nation, defeating their own almost-orthodox John Adams. Five years later they suffered through two almost equally severe defeats. Henry Ware was elected Hollis Professor of Divinity at Harvard College in the fall of 1805. And in the spring of 1806 Samuel Webber was elected Harvard's President. Both men were well-known Unitarians. While Harvard has long been suspected of heretical leanings, nothing so ominous had happened before. David Tappan, the Hollis Professor from 1792 until his death in 1803, was a moderate Calvinist who was trusted to provide an adequate theological education for evangelical ministers. And acting president Eliphalet Pearson (1804-06) was clearly one of the evangelicals whom they had hoped would succeed to the presidency of the college. Now the Commonwealth's proud old school had moved toward irremediable heresy. Clearly a crisis was at hand.

Pearson resigned in protest from the Harvard faculty and was welcomed to the village of Andover as the likely leader of a movement of resistance against the Unitarian incursion into New England's faith. By July, Pearson, Jedidiah Morse of Charlestown, and Samuel French of Andover, along with several prominent lay evangelicals, were meeting to develop a new institution as a counterbalance to the wayward school in Cambridge. The plan was to graft a clergy training institution onto Phillips Academy, Andover.

The planners of the new institution had much in their favor. Both Pearson and Morse were respected leaders of the Orthodox cause and could command support. The founders of Phillips

Academy had considered the training of ministers important and had already included provision for such work in the charter of their academy, although it is doubtful they had ever envisioned the sort of institution now developing.[7] The necessary funds were also available. A Boston merchant, Samuel Abbot, who had planned to leave his very sizeable fortune to Harvard for theological training, now transferred his interest and energy to the new project. It was an auspicious start for a new school.[8]

The Andover evangelicals were not, however, the only ones responding to the crisis in this way. The Rev. Samuel Spring of Newburyport and the Rev. Leonard Woods of West Newbury had been contemplating the creation of a school of theology for their adjoining parishes since 1801, and in 1806 they began to meet with some of the wealthy laymen of their churches to develop a plan. The two schools, one at Andover and the other at West Newbury, would be only a few miles apart.

Neither group had yet conceived of the sort of school which Andover would shortly become. Spring and Woods apparently foresaw a "Theological Academy" which would, in effect, continue the method of reading divinity which had been standard practice among New England clergy for more than a century—a pattern in which a college graduate spent from a few months to a couple of years studying theology in the home of a respected minister before seeking ordination.

No one spoke of more than a single faculty member, and in the case of the Newbury school, Woods as professor of divinity would also continue as a pastor, not unlike all who supervised the reading of divinity in parishes before him. Perhaps the new wealth available would have been used to acquire larger libraries. Or maybe Woods could have hired an assistant for his parish or Andover, a fulltime professor of divinity, so that the students could have their teacher's undivided attention. There is no indication that in early 1806 anyone had any other perspective. New possibilities were yet to emerge.

Shortly after some of the discussions in Newburyport, Leonard Woods went to Charlestown, Massachusetts, to discuss his work on the *Panopolist*, an evangelical journal, with its editor, Jedidiah Morse. In the course of the meeting, he happened to mention the plans for the Newbury Seminary. "This information," Wood records, "under the circumstances, almost overwhelmed him with a deep sense of the wonderful providence of God."[9] Morse quickly convinced the Newbury pastor of the desirability of a united institution, and the two began to work toward that end.

Merger would not be easy, however. The evangelicals of Massachusetts had internal divisions of their own. The Newbury followers were largely disciples of Samuel Hopkins. They saw themselves as the true heirs of the New England Puritans, Jonathan Edwards and his student Samuel Hopkins. All others, including the Andover Calvinists, were considered to be backsliders. Meanwhile at Andover, the old Calvinists (as they were known) considered their colleagues to the east to be extremists who had carried Calvinism to its most absurd conclusions. Both were heirs of the Great Awakening. Both supported revivals. And each side distrusted the other.[10]

From the spring of 1807 to the spring of 1808 Woods and Morse worked tirelessly to bring the rest of their reluctant colleagues along. Finally, working behind the scenes, Woods convinced the Newburyport lay donors that merger was desirable and presented Spring with a *fait accompli*.[11] In May 1808 the carefully-crafted compromise was presented to the Trustees of Phillips Academy, and plans were made to open Andover Theological Seminary in September as a united institution including the endowments and faculty of each of the schools. The need to unite in the face of the larger Unitarian threat and the opportunity to build something new in American education had won out.[12]

While the delicate negotiations on the governance of the institution and the faith of the faculty moved forward, plans were also progressing on the shape of the institution. Clearly there were resources here for something new in the training of clergy. Jedidiah Morse seems to have been the first to grasp the scope of the opportunity. In response to a fear voiced by Nathaniel Emmons that ministers from a theological college would not command as much respect as those with university degrees, Morse wrote, "Call not the Institution a College but a Theological Seminary. The idea is to admit young men into this school who have received education at some one of our Colleges."[13]

Andover would not compete with Harvard at the baccalaureate level—there were enough trusted colleges to do that—but would rather provide post-baccalaureate education for those entering the ministry. Morse's letter represents the first known use of the term *theological seminary* among American Protestants to denote theological schooling at this level. It was also one of the first attempts to plan a truly post-graduate professional school in the nation.

Shortly thereafter Morse wrote of the second unique characteristic at Andover: "It is to be on a broad foundation, and to have three Professors at least."[14] Not only would the school be a graduate institution, it would also have a faculty of more than one. No such graduate institution yet existed in the United States.

In speaking of the new institution's future, Timothy Dwight of Yale praised the donors "who have thus evangelically testified, that God has not showered wealth upon them in vain."[15] Whatever the original source of the wealth, the amount was indeed unusual for the endowment of any school at the time. Three donors from Andover and three from Newburyport gave the school $75,000 before it opened, and within their lives brought the amount to a full $300,000. In addition they provided, at their own expense, new buildings on the Andover campus to house the school and new houses in the town for the faculty.[16] At a time when Harvard's full endowment was about $150,000[17] this amount of money—twice Harvard's—meant that Andover had the potential freedom to experiment. It would be a long time before another seminary began with such unlimited opportunities.

To the great delight of orthodox New England, Andover Seminary opened on September 28, 1808. The patriarch of the evangelical movement, Timothy Dwight, journeyed up from New Haven to preside at the opening ceremonies. Jedidiah Morse closed the celebration announcing "A new era in our Churches now commences....A new institution..rises to bless our country."[18]

The opening of the seminary brought one more surprise to the founders. Woods wrote that "before the Seminary was organized, Dr. Spring expressed the hope that we should, in due time, have twelve or fifteen students in the Seminary at once."[19] Nineteen were waiting for admission when the school opened. The following year thirty-six were admitted, and numbers of that sort continued to come, with the result that the average student body, in three classes, was from the beginning around one hundred. Such large numbers contributed in ways unanticipated by the founders to shaping the new institution.

As it developed from the early plans of Morse, Woods, and others, and as it was reshaped through the experimentation of the early faculty, a coherent form of theological education took shape at Andover. Morse's plea for a post-college institution with at least three professors was the base. The students were also expected to stay three years to complete the curriculum. Woods summarized the program:

> A variety of methods were introduced and tried by the Professors, but after a few years it was agreed that the department of Sacred Literature should occupy the substance of the first year, Christian Theology, including Natural Theology, the second year; and the departments of Sacred Rhetoric and Ecclesiastical History the third year.[20]

This in sum was the model for theological education which would wield such influence in American Protestantism.

What was in the minds of those who put the school together? Of course, the pattern of reading divinity had been used in New England for a century, and the expansion of such a program into a small academy may well have been the initial goal of both groups. Spring already had been a mentor for some candidates. And the Andover Academy's bequest had provided rooms in the academy and some support for a dozen scholars who had studied in that parish.[21]

The ideal of a thorough education for the ministry, which included a liberal arts education followed by theological study, was common among most European Protestants and Catholics and had been carried over to the new world. This ordering of studies had been practiced in continental universities since the Renaissance and in Catholic minor and major seminaries since the Council of Trent. The anti-Catholicism of the evangelicals, along with the condition of Catholic theological education in the early 1800s, probably rules out the possibility of any Catholic influence on Andover, however. Also, in the early nineteenth century the distinction between the study of the classics in the minor seminaries and the study of philosophy and theology in the major seminaries was blurred among American Catholics where the church and its institutions were yet in embryonic form.[22] Certainly none of the Andover founders made any reference to Catholic models, either in public documents or private correspondence.

It is not clear, however, why the Andover founders adopted a three year program or how they settled on the substance of studies. The English universities, as well as Harvard and Yale, had required three years' study beyond a bachelor's degree for the honors of a master's degree. There was, however, no set curriculum for this program and some read divinity on campus or with a pastor, while others claimed that they merely had to survive for three years to collect the advanced degree.[23] The time requirements of master's honors may have been a factor in the decision for a three-year course of studies, but it could not have indicated the content or structure of those studies.

More suggestive is the little-known experiment of the small Associate Reformed Presbyterian Church, whose General Synod adopted a plan for a seminary in 1804 and opened the school in New York City in 1805. The plan called for a four-year curriculum including Biblical and theological studies. The school's curriculum was described in glowing terms in Morse's *Panoplist* in 1806. But the whole Associate Reformed curriculum was under the direction of a single professor, John Mitchell Mason, and for most of its students took the place of both college and seminary. If anything, "Mason's Seminary," as it was known, was probably the model for the "Theological College" which Nathaniel Emmons felt might not win sufficient respect for Andover.[24]

While all of these factors may have had a limited influence, none of them was decisive. Rather, Andover was indeed something new. The Andover plan was developed through experimentation in the first few years of operation. The arrival of a much larger student body than expected meant that the informality of many previous arrangements would not work. Certain teaching methods and curricular arrangements seem to have been tried and abandoned. But within a very few years, Woods and his two new colleagues Moses Stuart and Ebenezer Porter all seem to have agreed on the most desirable arrangement. In sum, the dissatisfaction with the ministerial education provided at Harvard, the insistence on doing something, the willingness to experiment, the availability of large sums of money and the unexpected numbers of students, all attributable in part to the energy released by the Second Great Awakening, had created something new in American education.

While they were willing to alter their program for ministerial education, the Andover faculty stood firm about admissions standards. Four requirements were consistently announced: piety—meaning conversion or belief in one's preparedness for conversion, a college education or its equivalent, moral character, and membership in a Christian church.[25] All requirements were taken seriously. Adoniram Judson, later to gain fame as a missionary to Burma, was admitted to the first class only provisionally because his piety was felt to be lacking.[26] But at the heart of the academic curriculum was the assumption that it was for college graduates. And the Andover faculty knew the sort of college curriculum they wanted. When Yale College, in 1828, adopted its famed "Yale Report" recommending the importance of a classical education as the basis for colleges,[27] many saw it as a reactionary move. For the Andover faculty, it was confirmation of what they had long been seeking. They only pleaded that Hebrew be added to the responsibilities of the colleges so that seminary years might not be consumed by language study.[28]

Written in response to a request that Yale drop the requirement of the "dead" languages, the "Yale Report" affirmed the need for the classical languages and literature—Latin and Greek—in a college education. "The object" according to the Yale faculty, "is not to *finish* his education; but to lay the foundation, and to advance as far in rearing the superstructure, as the short period of his residence here will admit."[29] Then in graduate work the specific skills of a profession could be acquired.

The "Yale Report" was conservative in its reaffirmation of the traditional classical curriculum as the core of the college's program. Yet it also represented a marked departure from the colonial college. Now college work was viewed as preparation for further studies. A college education was not necessarily complete in itself, but ideally provided the foundation for advanced work, probably in law, medicine, or theology, after which the candidate was truly prepared for life's work. This shift was itself due, in no small part, to the emergence of the Andover model of professional school in the preceding twenty years.

The requirement of a college degree was successfully maintained. Between its opening in 1808 and 1836 Andover received 693 students. Only forty-two did not hold a bachelor's degree.[30] The Andover model called for not only the three years of seminary work, but four years of college; the four/three pattern still in use today.

From the beginning most knowledgeable observers assumed that Leonard Woods would be the professor of theology at Andover. He served as the Abbot Professor for Christian Theology until his retirement in 1847. During the long tenure he taught Calvinism to generations of future preachers and missionaries while also attaining the reputation as a major defender of that tradition. If anything symbolized Andover's commitment to ensuring the orthodoxy of the next generation of ministers, it was the school's support of this doughty champion of orthodox Calvinism. Wood's debates with Henry Ware brought the differences between the orthodox and the Unitarians into focus, just as his more friendly debates with Lyman Beecher and Nathaniel William Taylor symbolized the differences emerging within the evangelical camp itself. In none of these discussions was Woods likely to compromise his own views.[31]

To no one's surprise Eliphalet Pearson was appointed Professor of Sacred Literature. He served, however, for only one year, resigning to concentrate his efforts on behalf of the seminary in his office as chairman of the trustees.[32] Pearson's successor was the thirty-year-old Moses Stuart, the popular pastor of New Haven's Center Church. At the time of his appointment, Stuart knew neither Hebrew, nor the German in which most existing Hebrew grammars were published. He would learn.

According to most accounts of the era of Andover's founding "the study of oriental languages and history was at a low ebb in New England. Even the study of Hebrew had fallen into almost total neglect."[33] Stuart set out to teach himself Hebrew. In the process, he realized that the best information on the subject was then available in German, and so he learned that language also. Indeed, his devotion to German scholarship and his encouraging of bright students to share this interest elicited more than a little distrust on the part of many of his supporters.[34] It also, however, helped to establish a pattern of connections between German and American higher education which was to grow in significance for the next century, introducing German research and teaching methods to the United States.

Stuart, in effect, set out to create a new academic field. His first published grammar was available in 1813, and his *Hebrew Grammar* of 1821 became the standard seminary text.[35] He not only created texts, he created a profession. After extra work at Andover, some of Stuart's students even made the trip to Germany for further study. When the American Oriental Society was established in 1849, the roll of membership published in its first *Journal* numbered sixty-eight scholars, twenty-three of whom were once pupils of Stuart.[36]

While Stuart and Woods dominated the intellectual life of Andover during its first four decades, the curriculum was also supposed to include Sacred Rhetoric and Ecclesiastical History. A famous preacher, Edward Door Griffin of Newark, New Jersey, was persuaded to accept the dual roles of teaching rhetoric at Andover Seminary and serving as pastor of the Park Street Church in Boston in 1809. He was well-liked by his colleagues and students, but quickly found the joint position more than he could carry. He resigned from Andover in 1811 to devote all his time to the Park Street congregation. As with Sacred Literature, the second appointment was to be more successful. Ebenezer Porter served Andover from 1812 till his death in 1834. He became as well-known for his published lectures on rhetoric as for his "Letters on Revivals." In 1827 Porter was also made President of the Seminary. In addition to his role as presiding officer at faculty meetings, he seems to have been primarily responsible for student discipline, a matter the more scholarly Stuart and Woods were happy to leave to Porter.[37]

The fourth department of the seminary, Ecclesiastical History, had a more checkered story. When money became available for a fourth position in 1819, Andover appointed James Murdock with responsibility in both the fields of rhetoric and history. It was an unhappy move. Although initially recommended by Woods, Murdock spent most of the next decade fighting with this three colleagues over his right to teach history and the place of ecclesiastical history in the seminary curriculum. Apparently the majority of the faculty had serious reservations about the importance of historical study. Finally, in 1828 the unhappy Murdock was forced off the faculty. The trustees redefined the fourth position as the "Brown Professorship of Pastoral Theology and Ecclesiastical History." The incumbent was both to teach history and to introduce students to the more practical affairs of church life.[38] These four departments constituted the Andover faculty until well after the Civil War. They also represent the general division of most seminary faculties to the present day.

The professors developed the methods of instruction, like the curriculum, by trial and error. Woods recorded that he began by giving all lectures in theology, but in time modified the system to allow for more class discussion. Like many of his successors, he complained about the problems of the few students who tended to dominate a discussion and the majority who "kept back by diffidence from joining in...." "My endeavors in this respect," he remembered after a forty-year struggle with the problem, "were successful only in part." Finally, in response to a student complaint that student presentations all tended to be the same, and therefore boring, Woods instituted a new exercise of having students submit written papers on which the professor commented, in writing. "The business of examining and criticizing so many dissertations proved to be very laborious," Woods noted, "but the students regarded it as promotive of their best improvement."[39]

The role of the Trustees and Visitors was limited. In a situation such as the Murdock crisis, they did indeed step in to settle the affair. The appointment of a president for the faculty in the midst of this debacle suggests, however, that the trustees did not want to become personally involved in the vicissitudes of faculty meetings.[40] On the other hand, the trustees never relaxed their vigilance about the orthodoxy of the faculty. When Leonard Woods published an implied criticism of the Westminster Confession, he was taken to task and modified his views. Far from complaining about this implied threat to his academic freedom, Woods expressed his gratitude to the trustees for rescuing him from "mistakes and inconsistencies." His only complaint was that they should have acted sooner.[41]

John E. Todd, an Andover student in the early 1820s, described student life in the institution in a letter to a friend:

> As you may suppose, I am buried up in theology. I am much driven in study. My class recites three times a week in theology, once in Hebrew, once in Greek, and attends three lectures, sometimes four. Besides this I belong to four different societies which meet evenings. In addition to this, I have now the appointment of writing a dissertation of one hour in length, to be delivered before the Society of Inquiry, respecting missions.[42]

Todd's life appears to have been fairly typical of student life as it developed at the seminary. Class work, student societies, and concerns with the state of their souls dominate the correspondence of Andover students. In addition, most were involved in some capacity with a church or a school to earn additional money, and in the early days they often worked in the seminary shop, for both exercise and spending money.

Rooted in the awakening, the early Andover kept the revival at the center of all its activity. The minister, as seen at Andover, was first of all a revivalist, and the purpose of the faculty was to produce more successful revivalists. To this end, the faculty created the Wednesday evening prayer conference.[43] Woods noted:

> Never can I forget those solemn and delightful seasons, when I went to the Conference Room with Professor Stuart, or with another of my beloved colleagues, and from the fulness of our hearts spoke to our pupils on the great principles of our holy religion, both doctrinal, experimental and practical. Many a time did Professor Stuart say to me, "If we do good in any way it is in this Conference."[44]

The conference was the one seminary exercise absolutely closed to outsiders. Here, with as much honesty as they could muster, students and teachers shared their concern and doubt over the state of their souls and for the evangelical movement. Often the conference centered on a topic of importance to future ministers— how they would conduct revivals, how they would govern their own lives in the pastorate, how the seminary curriculum did or did not help them.

Equally important to the students were the societies which they conducted with little aid from the faculty. There were many, as William Hallock, a member of the class of 1822 recorded:

> I am a little burdened with societies—Secretary of the Rhetorical, Secretary and Treasurer of the Lockhart Musical Society, Treasurer of the Auxiliary Corben, and Committee of Recommendation, Purchasing Committee of the Atheneum, Vice-President of the Society of Inquiry, treasurer of another society, agent also for purchasing German books. They do not all make a great demand, but they occupy some hours every week.[45]

If Hallock's schedule was somewhat unusual, nevertheless these societies did represent the point where the students took the most responsibility for their own theological education. And in all student memoirs they represent an important part of it.

The most important organization was the Society of Inquiry for Missions, which included virtually the whole student body. Here students searched their own hearts as to their call to the mission field, either on the western frontier or in some distant land. They also worked together to learn about missions. The societies carried on a vast correspondence with missionaries, and in time with the sister societies in other seminaries. Although faculties might fight over their theological differences, students in the Society of Inquiry kept themselves posted on developments and commitments to the mission field across the range of theological opinion.

From the outset the founding of Andover Seminary created a stir in the American Protestant religious world. Now other religious bodies seeking to define their own responses to the Second Great Awakening and to strengthen their programs for training ministers had a lead to follow. The Andover plan was adaptable and the basic idea of a three-year, three or four-professor, post-college theological seminary would indeed be used for many different ends.

Certainly the founders of Andover did all in their power to make sure that their model was widely emulated. A year after giving his blessing to the original school, Yale's President, Timothy Dwight, was in Philadelphia urging the Presbyterian General Assembly to adopt the plan, something that church did four years later—founding Princeton Theological Seminary in 1812.[46]

Most important to the spread of the Andover model of ministerial training was the work of the American Education Society. Established in Boston in the summer of 1815, the American Education Society (AES) along with its auxiliaries was to become the largest and most prominent organization providing scholarships for indigent ministerial students in the first half of the nineteenth century. Eliphalet Pearson, president of Andover's board of trustees, along with two faculty members, Ebenezer Porter and Moses Stuart, drafted the society's constitution.[47] The goal was to ensure a steady supply of ministers educated in the Andover mold. After 1828 this policy was very explicit: the society would aid only those candidates who would promise to "pursue a regular *three year course of theological study.*"[48]

Between 1815 and 1860 the AES aided nearly five thousand candidates for the ministry, or about one-quarter of all who attended seminary during that period.[49] The incentives to meet the society's requirements were strong. None of the successor seminaries to Andover had anything approaching its financial base. Most were small, harassed by debt, and eager to receive students who were fully financed. In one case, Bangor Seminary initially had sought to model itself on the four-year English dissenting academies which combined college and seminary rather than on the Andover plan. The AES recommended that the "institution should without much delay assume the character and rank of a purely *Theological Seminary,* adopt a three years course of Theological study, and carry the students through it in the usual way..."[50] The Bangor faculty sought to defend their system, but the Society was adamant and Bangor was in desperate financial straits. Within a year the trustees announced: "This Seminary has now assumed a form corresponding with that of other Theological Seminaries of our country."[51] The Andover model and the AES had won. The same story was repeated in several other cases. A surprising variety of schools were willing to make sure that their curriculum fit the ideal of the powerful society to benefit from its considerable largess.

At a crucial time the American Educational Society wielded tremendous influence in the spread of the three-year seminary, new in 1808, yet duplicated in dozens of schools in all regions and denominations before the Civil Way. Although the vast majority of Protestant clergy still engaged in other forms of education, within half a century every denomination had at least one school modeled on Andover which made the seminary an option for at least some of its candidates. And a good bit of the credit for this development must go to the unique agency which self-consciously set out to project its plan for theological education originating in Massachusetts Congregationalism on all parts of Protestant America.

The Andover faculty and trustees had a clear sense of being pacesetters and took pride in their position of leadership. Looking back on his own career, Woods wrote, "It is one of the most remarkable consequences of the establishment of this Institution, and one of the clearest proofs of the great value attached to it by the community, that so many similar Institutions have in so short a time been founded."[52] Speakers at Andover's Fiftieth Anniversary exercises echoed the same pride in their school as the "original type."[53]

Nurtured by the energy of the awakening, supported by generous donors, attracting an able faculty and student body, Andover Theological Seminary itself emerged in the decades after 1806 as a new type of institution for theological education. Although copied by many, the original school at Andover, Massachusetts, would remain, throughout the nineteenth century, as a beacon, attracting some of the best students and sending forth faculty members for similar institutions and notable missionaries and ministers for the American churches. Andover was imitated as an institutional model by many who did not accept its understanding of the nature of the ministry, but Andover was founded and operated out of a very clear view of the minister as a scholarly, orthodox, revivalist.

FOOTNOTES

[1] Charles Roy Keller, *The Second Great Awakening in Connecticut* (New Haven: Yale University Press, 1942), pp. 37-38.

[2] Barton Warren Stone, *The Biography of Eld. Barton Warren Stone, written by himself: with Additions and Reflections by Elder John Rogers* (Cincinnati: J.A. & U.P. James, 1847), p. 38.

[3] Vincent Harding, "Lyman Beecher and the Transformation of American Protestantism, 1775-1863" (Ph.D. dissertation, University of Chicago, 1965), pp. 37ff., and Sidney Earl Mead, *Nathaniel William Taylor, 1786-1856, A Connecticut Liberal* (Chicago: The University of Chicago Press, 1942), p. 41.

[4] Timothy Dwight, "The Nature and Danger of Infidel Philosophy, Exhibited in Two Discourses, Addressed to the Candidates for the Baccalaureate, in Yale College," September 9, 1797 (New Haven: Printed by George Bunce, 1798).

[5] For a more detailed study of this cluster of institutions see my *Pedagogue for God's Kingdom: Lyman Beecher and the Second Great Awakening*, (Lanham, MD: University Press of America, 1985).

[6] Leonard Woods, *History of the Andover Theological Seminary* (Boston: James R. Osgood and Co., 1885), p. 27.

[7] See James McLachlan, *American Boarding Schools: A Historical Study* (New York: Charles Scribner's Sons, 1970) pp. 40-42.

[8] See Leonard Woods, pp. 47-132; also John H. Giltner, "The Fragmentation of New England Congregationalism and the Founding of Andover Seminary," *Journal of Religious Thought* 20 (1963-64): 27-42.

[9] Woods, p. 77.

[10] Leonard Bacon, *A Commemorative Discourse on the Completion of Fifty Years* (Andover: Draper, 1858), p. 15. Bacon's speech is the best analysis available of the differences between the two parties. Henry K. Rowe, *History of Andover Theological Seminary* (Newton, Massachusetts: Thomas Todd Company, 1933) thoroughly confuses the issues.

[11] Woods, p. 90.

[12] See the example Frank Dixon McCloy, "The Founding of Protestant Theological Seminaries in the United States of America, 1784-1840" (Ph.D. dissertation, Harvard University, 1959), pp. 142-44.

[13] "Jedidiah Morse to Leonard Woods, October 21, 1806," in William B. Sprague, *The Life of Jedidiah Morse, D.D.* (New York: Anson D.F. Randolph &

Company, 1874), p. 97.

[14] "Jedidiah Morse to Charles Taylor, December 23, 1806," in Sprague, pp. 97-98.

[15] Timothy Dwight, " A Sermon Preached at the Opening of the Theological Institution in Andover; and at the Ordination of Rev. Eliphalet Pearson, Ll.D.," September 28, 1808 (Boston: Farrand, Mallory, and Co., 1808), p. 23.

[16] Woods, pp. 139-40.

[17] Josiah Quincy, *History of Harvard University*, 2 vols. (Cambridge: John Owen, 1840), 2:558.

[18] Jedidiah Morse, "The Right Hand of Fellowship," preached with and bound with Dwight's "Sermon," p. 35.

[19] Woods, p. 137.

[20] Ibid., p. 186.

[21] Ibid., p. 49; MacLachlan, p. 35.

[22] John Tracy Ellis, "From Trent to the 1960's," *Essays in Seminary Education* (Notre Dame, Indiana: Fides Publishers, Inc., 1967), pp. 41-111.

[23] Samuel Eliot Morison, *Harvard College in the Seventeenth Century*, 2 vols. (Cambridge: Harvard University Press, 1936), 1: 272-80.

[24] For an excellent study of "Mason's Seminary," see Frank Dixon McCloy, "John Mitchell Mason: Pioneer in American Theological Education," *Journal of Presbyterian History* 44 (September, 1966): 141-55. For an older history of the school see "The History, Catalogue, and Arrangements of the Theological Seminary of the Associate Reformed Synod of New York, at Newburg: to which is added the Address of the Rev. J. McCarrell, D.D. at the opening of the session, 1839-1840: (Newburg: J.D. Spalding, n.d., ca. 1839).

[25] Ebenezer Porter, "Terms of Admission to the Theological Seminary, Andover," *The American Quarterly Register* 5 (August, 1832): 93-94.

[26] Woods, pp. 136-37.

[27] Published as "Original Papers in Relation to a Course of Liberal Education," *The American Journal of Science and Arts* 15 (January, 1839): 297-351. Hereafter cited as Yale Report.

[28] Moses Stuart to the Secretary of the American Education Society, *The Quarterly Register and Journal of the American Education Society* 8 (April, 1829): 193-204.

[29] Yale Report, p. 308.

[30] *The American Quarterly Register* 9 (May, 1837): 375.

[31] Leonard Bacon, "Commemorative Discourse," in *A Memorial of the Semi-Centennial Celebration of the Founding of the Theological Seminary at Andover* (And Warren F. Draper, 1859).

[32] Woods, p. 186.

[33] Charles C. Torrey, "The Beginnings of Oriental Study at Andover," *The American Journal of Semitic Languages and Literatures* 13 (July, 1897): 249.

[34] See for example Theodore Davenport Bacon, *Leonard Bacon: A Statesman*

in the Church (New Haven: Yale University Press, 1931), p. 45.

[35] Torrey, pp. 254-55.

[36] Ibid., p. 264.

[37] Woods, pp. 181-85; see also "Rev. Ebenezer Porter, D.D. Late President of the Theological Seminary, Andover," *The Quarterly Register* 9 (August, 1836): 9-16.

[38] J. Earl Thompson, "Church History Comes to Andover: The Persecution of James Murdock," *Andover Newton Quarterly* 15 (March, 1975): 223. This article gives a very detailed account of the controversy.

[39] Woods, pp. 159-63.

[40] Ibid., p. 182.

[41] Ibid., pp. 180-81.

[42] John Todd, John Todd: *The Story of His Life*, ed. John E. Todd (New York: Harper & Brothers, 1876), p. 102.

[43] Rowe, p. 50.

[44] Woods, p. 164.

[45] Mrs. H.C. Knight, *Memorial of Rev. Wm. A. Hallock, D.D.* (New York: American Tract Society, n.d.), pp. 17-18.

[46] *Extracts from the Minutes of the General Assembly of the Presbyterian Church in the United States of America; A.D. 1809* (Philadelphia: Jane Aitken, 1809).

[47] Natalie Ann Naylor, "The American Education Society, 1815-1860," (Ed.D. dissertation, Teachers College, Columbia University, 1971). Naylor's dissertation is a very useful study of the AES. Also helpful is David F. Allmendinger, Jr., *Paupers and Scholars, the Transformation of Student Life in Nineteenth Century New England* (New York: St. Martin's Press, 1975).

[48] "Quarterly Meeting of the Directors," *Quarterly Register* 1 (January, 1828): 55-56.

[49] Naylor, p. 90.

[50] Ibid., p. 203.

[51] Ibid., p. 205-6.

[52] Woods, p. 201.

[53] Bacon, "Commemorative Discourse," p. 104.

47

Chapter III
NOT FLATTERING THE PROUD,
BUT PLEADING THE CAUSE OF THE POOR

ABOLITIONISM, ACTIVISM, AND THE FOUNDING
OF OBERLIN COLLEGE

Among the theological seminaries which were founded along the lines laid down at Andover, one was to be the scene of one of the most spectacular debates in the nineteenth century about the nature of the ministry. In the fall of 1834, the majority of the students at the newly formed Lane Theological Seminary in Cincinnati, Ohio withdrew from the institution to search for a new school. They left, they said, because they believed that the trustees and faculty—led by an aging Lyman Beecher—were interfering with their freedom to live out the Christian gospel by restricting their abolitionist activities. These students sought a theological education "in which we should accomplish vastly more for the salvation of men, than we should by being entirely enervated in the soul chilling atmosphere of a popular institution where to gain the art of *pleasing* rather than *saving* men is the standard of excellence."[1]

In their parting statement, the students, led by Theodore Dwight Weld, voiced an activist model of ministry as it was emerging in their era. For these students, ministers and seminary students should be those who are "not parleying with wrong, but calling it to repentance; not flattering the proud, but pleading the cause of the poor..."[2] For these students the minister was neither primarily orthodox scholar nor converted

49

saver of individual souls, but an activist engaged in the struggle to build a better, more Christian civilization on the American continent. The Lane debates have been interpreted in many ways.[3] For Beecher they were a series of errors. For Weld they were one more battle in the war for abolition. They were, indeed, both of these things, and many more, but they were also a debate between different generations of ministers and, more important, different conceptions for the Christian ministry.

Lane Theological Seminary which began its first classes in the Cincinnati, Ohio suburb of Walnut Hills in the fall of 1832 was a strange hybrid. The school was originally founded by old school Presbyterians whose roots were in Virginia and Kentucky and who had migrated to Cincinnati at least a decade before Weld or Beecher. As early as 1822, Joshua L. Wilson, a native of Virginia who would emerge as one of the leaders of the anti-revivalist old school Presbyterians, was serving as pastor of the First Presbyterian Church in Cincinnati. Wilson proposed a seminary for the "western section of the Presbyterian Church."[4]

By the time it opened, the school included not only westerners, but also Lyman Beecher, a New England Congregationalist who had been one of the leaders of the interdenominational voluntary societies for missions, Sunday Schools, and Bible and tract distribution as President. It also included a student body, led by Theodore Dwight Weld, the majority of whom had been converted in the hot-bed of new school revivalism in upstate New York inspired by the preaching of Charles Grandison Finney. Finney began his ministry as a Presbyterian but went much farther then even Lyman Beecher in the new school direction of free will in both theology and church polity. Indeed, even before the Presbyterian Church split nationally between the new school and old school parties, Finney had given up on both to become an independent Congregationalist.

Lane's original founders, led by Joshua Wilson, were always ambivalent about the newcomers. Without them the school would have closed. Southern Ohio alone could not produce enough students or money to keep a seminary going. But the New England and New York immigrants also brought ideas in theology and politics which were very much at odds with the school's original goals.

Each of these groups brought conflicting understandings of the nature of the Christian ministry to the school. And at Cincinnati the ideas and the conflicts would develop with a clarity not previously seen. For Joshua Wilson, and for many of his old school colleagues, the role of a minister was to preach orthodoxy. The results of orthodoxy in building revivals, or in changing society, were quite secondary. Wilson's position was caricatured by Beecher's daughter, Harriet Beecher Stowe, "There are men—one or two, I mean—whose minds have been brought up in a catechetical tread-mill—who never say 'Confession of Faith' without taking off their hats, and who have altogether the appearance of thinking that the Bible is the *next best book* to the Catechism."[5] Stowe, like any good Beecher, could not understand such commitment to orthodox theology. But for Wilson, as for the majority of the old school, preaching the true faith was the heart of the ministry. The split between the old school and the new school in the Presbyterian church in the 1830s has been seen as a sectional split, a split regarding differing views on slavery, denominational control of missionary agencies, as well as differing interpretations of revivalism and Calvinism.[6] It was all of these things, but it was also a split regarding the understanding of the work of the Christian minister. And it must be viewed in this light also.[7]

For Lyman Beecher, the minister's role was quite different from Wilson's. The minister, Beecher believed, was to lead a revival, and the revival was to lead to the development of a range of church-related organizations which would change society. Thus, Beecher described his own approach to theology as that of a physician who, "would go to the store of the apothecary [for remedies] to be applied...."[8] Such an approach to theology, picking one doctrine here and another there to deal with a particular situation, made little sense to Wilson. But Beecher's goal was not right theology as such, but right action—action in the experience of conversion, and action in the building of a new society. Again, Beecher's daughter caught the core of his commitment in ministry, "A sermon that did not induce any body to *do any thing* he considered a sermon thrown away.."[9] Others might preach to change people's minds, Beecher preached to change people's actions. This was an

51

activism the old school could not understand or tolerate.

For Charles Finney or Theodore Weld, however, Beecher's moves simply did not go far enough. Both Finney and Weld were true radicals, going to what they believed was the heart of the Christian gospel, and then proclaiming that gospel, and its implications for society, without fear of the results. In this way they were closer to Wilson. Neither Wilson nor Finney could tolerate Beecher's willingness to compromise. Because of their understanding of the nature of the ministry—and of ministerial activism—neither Finney or Weld had any patience for Beecher's commitment to Presbyterian unity. Let the old school go. Let half of the new school and their New England Congregationalist allies go. The minister's work was something else—a preacher calling sinners to conversion and calling a sinful nation and church to change. Throughout his career, Finney made this call from the revival pulpit, while Weld went further as a evangelist speaking for the antislavery cause. But for both, the role of the minister was to call sinners to immediate and total change. Church organization, and church unity, were definitely secondary.

Lyman Beecher's View of the Activist Minister

Many of Lyman Beecher's most serious struggles throughout his ministry were with those who distrusted the ways in which he was changing the definition of the ministry. Even before he went to Lane, Andover's President, Ebenezer Porter was warning him, "I regret the impression you have been making, because the grand danger of ministry always has been a tendency to modify the Gospel to appease opposition."[10] Wilson would certainly pick up the same charge in Cincinnati. Both Wilson and Porter saw the defense of orthodox theology as central to a minister's role. Beecher did not. Defending orthodoxy was always an adjunct to the minister's primary role as activist in the cause of revivals and social reform.

But activist though he was, Beecher's form of activism differed radically from that espoused by Theodore Dwight Weld and other Lane students. Indeed they were probably more different than they ever realized. Lyman Beecher focused on a mix of activities designed to reform society, to educate individual Christians and to return the nation—especially the western frontier—to a nostalgic vision of the New England town of Beecher's youth.[11] Weld had no such nostalgia. On the contrary, his focus was on sin, and in his own generation the power of a particular sin—chattel slavery. Until the radical change of abolition took place, no reform, especially no reform which returned the nation to an earlier, simpler way, could do anything except perpetuate evil.

When Lyman Beecher came to Cincinnati and the Lane presidency in 1832 he already had behind him a long career as an activist minister. Born in Connecticut in 1775, graduated from Yale in 1797, and licensed to preach in 1798, Beecher had been a New England pastor first at East Hampton, Long Island, later at Litchfield, Connecticut and then at Boston, Massachusetts, and the organizer of a number of reform crusades. In his career, Beecher became the advocate for a new educational pattern in the American church. He urged a carefully controlled revival, a range of benevolent societies—for Sunday schools, missions, temperance, and education—and a variety of publications which would all work together to help transform the society. Whether he was preaching, organizing for one of the benevolent societies, or writing for publication, Beecher's goal remained consistent. He was a social reformer intent upon affecting the, "moral destiny of our nation."[12]

While he worked to transform society Beecher also helped to transform the nature of ministry. The ensuing changes may have been an unintended consequence of his work. Beecher did not focus his attention on the ministry per se, but one could not be involved in the flurry of activity which Beecher generated—corresponding with fellow reformers, attending meetings, gathering new recruits for his organizations—and still maintain the older New England tradition of the scholarly pastor spending many hours each day in the study.

Beecher did not begin this process of change. A generation earlier, his own mentor, Timothy Dwight, had been involved in similar activities, although on a much more modest scale. From Beecher's perspective, a new and active nation demanded a new kind of minister. The scholar-pastor might do great work but he would not participate in the struggle to convert the nation. To win that fight something new was needed in the ministry—an activist willing to take on the struggle of organizing for the millennium. Early in his career, Beecher had described his own interpretation of ministry, "I am sure that I exert a powerful and salutary influence out of the pulpit, in conference meeting, and lectures, and family visits, as I do in the pulpit on the Sabbath day."[13] By the 1830's. Beecher had become a model of this new kind of minister, as well as a well-known leader in the voluntary associations of the day and a speaker for the New England wing of American evangelicalism.

By this time, however, Beecher was ready to leave a successful Boston pastorate for a move to "Cincinnati, the London of the West...."[14] Like many other evangelicals, Beecher had come to believe that in the Mississippi Valley all of the contending forces which they saw on the American stage—their own, other Protestants, Catholics, and frontier secularists—were meeting afresh. And he wanted to be in the middle of that struggle which offered the winner a new opportunity to build "the city on a hill" on a larger and grander scale.

Thus, when Beecher was approached by Franklin Y. Vail, the agent for Lane Seminary, in the late fall of 1830 about becoming the school's first president his bags were virtually packed. He was inaugurated as Professor of Theology and President of Lane Seminary on December 26, 1832.

While serving as a seminary president was new to Beecher, an interest in theological education was not. Early in his own ministry, he had welcomed a young candidate for ministry Elias Cornelius, into his home to read divinity. In his letter to Cornelius, Beecher made it clear that action as well as reading would be part of Cornelius' theological education:

> I like your plan much of acquainting yourself with the active duties of a minister as well as with doctrinal knowledge. I hope the thing will be hereafter regarded, as the usefulness of a minister depends much upon the manner of presenting the truth, and upon his pastoral enterprise among his people.[15]

As early as 1815, Beecher's definition of a minister was an activist, who believed that future usefulness depended on the minister's "manner" and "enterprise" as much as on doctrinal knowledge. After all, his own theological education with Timothy Dwight had been given a similar focus. Beecher remembered the heart of the matter, "As to doctrines, we had his course of sermons, and were left pretty much to ourselves and our reading. Dwight was, however, a revival preacher, and a new era of revivals was commencing..."[16] An activist style of ministry, it seemed was part of Beecher's understanding of the profession from the beginning. Doctrines could be left for a secondary role.

Once he moved to Lane, Beecher intended to keep the same focus clear. He did not want to allow either himself or his students to be caught up in the study of theology without its application. He insisted that his own work as a seminary professor and president also include the pastorate of a church:

> I think it highly important that the theological instructor should, if possible, sustain the pastoral relation, and the students worship with him in a popular assembly—that while in the acquisition of doctrine they might witness its application, and feel its power, and observe its effect.[17]

And even after he retired from Lane, he criticized Andover Seminary for not following the same pattern.

> I considered that to take a man out of the ministry to make him a professor, without a congregation to keep him up by revival work he would run down spiritually, as they do here [written at Andover] and everywhere else. It would have been so with me if I had had nothing to do but to con over my lectures, so I took up the full responsibility of pastoral duty, as if I had had nothing else to do.[18]

His successor at Lane remembered the focus, "The students went forth from under this electric power over them determined, with the help of God to be revival preachers...."[19] That is certainly the way Beecher would have wanted it. The revival, and the wide range of activities which flowed from it were the heart of the ministry for him. The details of theology, which were so important to the old school, were simply part of the supportive framework for him.

In Cincinnati, Beecher was greeted by a student body of young men who had been converging on the Ohio campus throughout the late summer and fall of 1832. They, like their President, were committed to action. He described them with enthusiasm:

> Our first class is forty, and the large majority of it composed of men of matured age, powerful mind, and ardent and devoted piety. I have never known such power and intelligent and strong action condensed in a single class.[20]

The vast majority of the students, however, had not come to Lane because of Lyman Beecher. A different source of energy and ideas—including ideas about the proper role for a minister—came to the seminary from the revivalism of upstate New York which was led by Charles G. Finney.

Charles G. Finney and a Different Model of Ministry

Throughout the 1820s, Charles Grandison Finney had been emerging as the leading revivalist in New York. Converted under the preaching of the Presbyterian pastor in Adams, New York, George W. Gale, Finney left a successful law practice to begin his own career as a revivalist. Reminded of a pending case by one of his clients, Finney responded, "Deacon B____, I have a retainer from the Lord Jesus Christ to plead his cause, and I cannot plead yours."[21] For the next four decades, Finney would continue to plead the Lord's cause in America.

Already in 1827 Beecher and Finney had clashed over their differing styles of revivalism.[22] Beecher had accused Finney of creating too much controversy in a revival, stirring up too much emotion, and most seriously, refusing to follow the lead of the more established church people in New England. While they had effected something of a reconciliation, the next few years would find the differences between the two, both in personality and in basic understanding of the ministry, far too great to reconcile.

Among the things which Finney did not share with Beecher was Beecher's passion for schooling. Douglas M. Sloan has clarified the differences which were emerging between these two eastern evangelicals:

> Education and college founding, like other social reforms, were always valued by Finney for their service to revival religion....Lyman Beecher, by contrast, tended to view revivalism as a handmaiden to the spread and maintenance of civilization and its institutions.[23]

Having been converted and being convinced that he was called to preach, Finney wanted to preach, not study. In his own experience, Finney was impatient to get on with his work. He was also distrustful of the results of formal theological training. When his Presbytery began the steps toward his ordination in 1822,

> Some of the ministers urged me to go to Princeton to study theology, but I declined....and when urged to give them my reasons, I plainly told them that I would not put myself under such an influence as they had been under; that I was confident they had been wrongly educated, and they were not ministers that met my ideal of what a minister of Christ should be.[24]

While Finney's New York colleagues might have respected his blunt speaking, proper New Englanders like Beecher did not. His attacks on their institutions made them extremely wary.

Since they in turn did not trust many of the existing church institutions, Finney and his followers set out to create their own. In 1823, Finney's former pastor, George W. Gale, retired from the pastorate and founded the Oneida Manual Labor Institute, purchasing a farm in Whitesboro, New York in 1824. Gale's goal was to support Finney's cause by training his students. The Oneida Institute covered as much of a college and early seminary education in theology as possible in a limited amount of time. The students could then move on to more advanced work in college or theological seminary, or more likely directly into preaching.[25] But whatever they did, they were guaranteed an education at Oneida in an atmosphere completely supportive to Finney style revivalism.

A second goal for Gale's school was to keep the cost of education as low as possible.[26] In order to do this, students supported themselves working on the campus farm. A number of Finney converts began to attend the school, which by 1829—an exceptionally good harvest year—was prospering. The link of manual labor with Finney's style of theological education had thus begun as a form of improvisation, but quickly became a pattern which was copied elsewhere.[27]

Oneida was indeed an apt embodiment of Finney revivalism, combining as it did an abbreviated theological education with a strict moral regimen and physical work which was both morally and financially helpful. Equally important, manual labor became a symbol not only for New York revivalists, but especially for the abolitionists among them.

Among those studying at Oneida in 1829 was a recent Finney convert, Theodore Dwight Weld.[28] Weld had been converted during the Great Revival in Utica in 1825. He quickly became an important assistant to Finney, championed the right of women to speak in the revivals, and in 1827 began to study for the ministry. At Oneida, Weld became thoroughly convinced of the merits of the manual labor system. He also became even more convinced of the evil of slavery and the need for immediate emancipation if the conversion of the nation was ever to mean social rather than merely personal transformation.[29]

In 1831 the cause of manual labor received two significant boosts. Lewis Tappan, one of the leading philanthropists for a variety of evangelical activities, chiefly anti-slavery, joined with others to form the Society for Promoting Manual Labor in Literary Institutions. And Weld agreed to serve as the Society's agent. It could be a powerful combination—as it would be later in the anti-slavery cause—Tappan's money and Weld's energy and organizing ability.[30] Between 1831 and 1833, Weld traveled the nation promoting the system, raising funds, and recruiting students.

As agent for the Tappan society, Weld preached the manual labor cause and reported back to Tappan on the results. He was also commissioned to find a site for a national manual labor institution where the new method, supported by Tappan money, could be used to raise a generation of clergy who could combine Finney's evangelical style with anti-slavery organizing in the new west. Sites in western New York State and Ohio were considered.[31] Franklin Vail, who as Lane's agent would soon be involved in the negotiations to bring Lyman Beecher to the faculty, was naturally interested in this project, for it could spell both money and students for the struggling school. Late in 1831 he wrote to Weld asking him to consider Lane's location at the heart of the Mississippi Valley and,

> not to fix upon your location for this institution until you have paid a visit to this great valley, and have conferred with some brethren who have been looking over the rising millions of the West with a view of raising up just such an institution as you wish....[32]

As with Beecher, so for Weld, Lane Seminary happened to be in the right place at the right time. Weld recommended it as the location and the Tappan brothers accepted the recommendation. It was clearly a marriage of convenience. Although the Cincinnatians had added manual labor as something of an afterthought, they did have a charter and a location. And though the New Yorkers were not necessarily convinced that the manual labor school should be a post-college seminary, they had the Tappan money and were looking for a viable location. In spite of problems which would surface very quickly, the union was made.

At Lane the primary voice for the Finney style of ministry would be Theodore Weld, and he had the majority of students with him. In a letter to Weld, one student wrote, "My Dear Brother, we want you here immediately very much....Lane Seminary is only a beast without a head. True, Dr. Beecher is coming soon but he is not acquainted with manual labour-ism...."[33] Much of the correspondence between Weld and other students during the early months of the school reflects the same allegiance. Beecher would do well enough as president and professor of theology. But the real loyalty was to manual labor and abolitionism and Weld's leadership. The trustees were described as "*very fallible* men."[34]

Lane Seminary: The Point of Conflict

The three streams which merged at Lane Seminary between 1832 and 1834—the old school founders, the New Englander president, and the students who had come from the New York revivals— meant far more energy and far more secure funding for the school than any one group alone could have brought to the enterprise. They also meant that the seeds of serious discord were planted in Lane by the time it opened its doors to theological students. Perhaps only the seminary's dauntless agent, Franklin Vail, realized the diversity which was coming together. As he wrote to Weld from Cincinnati:

> Now, as we already have New England identified with this enterprise we only need to have your plan and efforts identified with our own, in order to secure the influence of New York, and make it strictly a national, model institution.[35]

Such a situation could produce the most fruitful sort of interchange on the new frontier, but it could also bring the most bitter sort of division.

The seminary's old school founders had already begun to doubt their move to include others by the time Beecher arrived. If the minister was, above all, to preach orthodoxy, then it was essential for the seminary professors to be orthodox. As early as 1832, some members of Cincinnati Presbytery wrote to Beecher that his theology was, "so variant from our solemn convictions of what the truth as it is in Jesus is, that we must, in all good conscience before God, enter our deliberate and prayerful dissent to your ministry among us."[36] This dissent would only grow.[37]

At the same time, the conflict between the new school Beecher and the old school members of the Cincinnati Presbytery was only a part of the backdrop for the conflict between Beecher and his students, led by Weld. Not long after his arrival at the seminary's campus, Theodore Dwight Weld wrote:

> I am deliberately, earnestly, solemnly, with my whole heart and soul and mind and strength, for the immediate, universal, and total abolition of slavery.[38]

60

Through Weld's influence, this position would quickly come to be shared by the majority of his fellow students.

Arthur and Lewis Tappan who had played such an important role in providing the funds to bring both Beecher and Weld to Lane shared Weld's position on this matter. Indeed, their commitment to immediate abolitionism was their primary reason for supporting the western institution. Lewis Tappan's biographer has correctly stated their expectations:

> With Tappan paying their expenses, Weld and an eager band from Oneida Academy joined Beecher at Walnut Hills, which overlooked Cincinnati, the Ohio River, and the Kentucky slaveland beyond. From this source at Lane, the Tappan brothers expected an anti-slavery tide to roll eastward.[39]

Lyman Beecher's position was more than a little different. To the surprise of his Tappan benefactors, he would not agree with their single-minded devotion to one cause. Beecher was a reconciler, but this very concern with reconciliation betrayed the very basic differences which existed between Beecher and Weld.[40] Beecher needed reconciliation between the most moderate and the most extreme abolitionists so that they could continue the larger campaign. For Weld there was no larger campaign. Righteousness was the issue. Thus while both Beecher and Weld used much of the same evangelical language, and while both advocated a form of ministry which was actively involved in the issues of the day, the two differed radically on the proper focus and purpose of that activity.

In an earlier day the two positions could have coexisted, as Beecher hoped they would. But concern about slavery was rising throughout the land. Compromise was increasingly difficult. Weld and his strongest allies quickly set about to convert the student body. They talked with fellow students, reasoned with them about their doubts, and produced evidence of the horror of slavery and the sin of slave holding. They did not call a meeting until they were sure of some public converts.

Finally for eighteen tumultuous evenings in February, 1834, the debates were held. Weld and his fellow students were well prepared and marshalled their arguments about the horrors of slavery and the need for immediate emancipation. At the

61

conclusion, nearly all of the Lane student body voted in favor of immediate abolitionism and against more gradual solutions to slavery.[41]

Activists that they were, the students did not stop with debate. As Weld wrote to Lewis Tappan a month later:

> We believe that faith without *works* is dead. We have formed a large and efficient organization for elevating the colored people in Cincinnati—have established a Lyceum among them, and lecture three or four evenings a week....Besides this, an evening free school, for teaching them to read, is in operation....[42]

Many of the trustees and the Cincinnati newspapers began to be very nervous and critical about this level of activism.[43]

Beecher, while not as cautious as the trustees, also feared that these well-intentioned activities by his students would make life impossible for the seminary.[44] Beecher, always a gradualist and a moderate, believed that united action by converted Christians would transform the nation. He did not want to risk that unity for an immediate reform which, in any case, he considered impossible of achievement.

With the coming of summer, Beecher and the rest of the faculty did not consider the controversy serious enough to warrant their missing the annual trip east to raise funds and plead the cause of western education. When, however, he visited the school's chief benefactors—the Tappans—Beecher found them completely sympathetic with the students. In spite of his attempts to convince the Tappan brothers that all was well at Lane, Lewis Tappan responded, "If you, doctor, were a thorough anti-slavery man, how easy it would be for you and Mr. Weld to go on harmoniously."[45] But Beecher's understanding of the minister's role made thorough commitment to any one cause impossible. This was the heart of his differences with Weld and the Tappans.

In October, 1834, when Beecher returned to Cincinnati, he "found all in a flurry."[46] The trustees had passed a resolution, "requiring that the Anti-Slavery Society and Colonization Society of the seminary be abolished."[47] In response, the students had left the campus. The students were still hopeful that Beecher would resign and join them. Instead he tried to negotiate a settlement.[48] But it was far too late, and the differences were far too great. In spite of Beecher's pleas, the students did not return. Instead from their temporary residence in Cumminsville, Ohio they issued their own final words on the affairs of Lane Seminary.

In a powerful statement, the students insisted that to achieve the necessary preparation for ministry they were led...

> to adopt this principle, *that free discussion, with correspondent effort is a* DUTY, *and of course a* RIGHT....We applied it to missions, at home and abroad; and we *acted* immediately. ...Next moral reform came up. We examined it, in a series of adjourned meetings; light was elicited, principles were fixed, and action followed. With the same spirit of free inquiry, we discussed the question of slavery.

But of course slavery caused a much more severe response from the authorities, until the students were led to say, "The ground of our succession from the Seminary, is, that free discussion and correspondent action have been prohibited by law." As long as Lane maintained a rule on its books which limited the students' right to do their duty as they saw it, they could not remain and be true to their understanding of who a minister should be. They concluded:

> Finally, we would respectfully remind the trustees, that men, though students of a theological seminary, should be treated as men,—that men, destined for the service of the world, need, above all things, in such an age as this, the pure and impartial, the disinterested and magnanimous, the uncompromising and fearless,—in combination with the gentle and tender spirit and example of Christ; not parleying with wrong, but calling it to repentance; not flattering the proud, but pleading the cause of the poor.[49]

It was the end of the debate. The differences between the different factions and different visions of the ministry were too clear and too significant for any reconciliation.

Oberlin: A School for Activists

Having left Lane Seminary, some of the Lane Rebels, as they became known, moved on to other things. Most of the group, however, remained together. Through the friendly support of Asa Mahan—the only Lane trustee to oppose the resolutions—and a few other Cincinnati natives--and aided as usual with liberal drafts on the Tappan brothers funds—the Lane students rented a house on the outskirts of the city and continued both their theological studies and their work among the Blacks of the city. For the 1834-35 school year this informal combination of theological study and activist ministry worked well. More permanent arrangements were developing, however.[50]

Lane Seminary was not the only struggling western school looking for energetic students and a liberal endowment. One of the more romantic attempts at college founding had been made by John J. Shipherd and Philo P. Stewart in the village of Oberlin, Ohio. They had chartered their Oberlin Collegiate Institute in 1832 and opened with two teachers and eleven students in 1833.[51] From the beginning, Oberlin's founders described their school as being "distinctive in its character." They described their design:

> Its grand object is the diffusion of useful science, sound morality, and pure religion....For this purpose it proposes as its primary object, the thorough education of ministers and pious School Teachers. As a secondary object, the elevation of female character. And as a third general design, the education of the *common people* with the higher classics in such a manner as suits the nature of Republican institutions.[52]

To accomplish these goals, the school developed a detailed plan of manual labor and a commitment to healthful, simple living. Oberlin was also the first school in the nation to admit women. The school was vaguely Presbyterian in orientation, although the neighboring Western Reserve College received most of the support which was available from Presbyterian sources.

For all its uniqueness, however, Oberlin was hardly a prospering venture. But during the year in which the Lane rebels

64

were on their own, Shipherd made contact with both the students and their Tappan benefactors. As with Lane three years earlier, it would be a fortuitous connection.

Agreements were reached through the year so that in the fall of 1835 the Lane Rebels simply became the new Theology Department at Oberlin. Unlike Lane, however, this time the students did not move into a situation of conflict. They simply took over the school.[53]

Neither Weld and the other students nor the Tappans were taking any chances on a repeat of the Lane experience. Before agreeing to move to Oberlin, the anti-slavery activists insisted that their friend from Cincinnati, Asa Mahan, must be elected president of the school and that Charles Grandison Finney be elected professor of theology. They also insisted that Blacks be admitted to the student body. Having met all of their demands, Shipherd met some resistance on his own board of trustees, but as with Lane, the prospect of students and money was more than the struggling school could reject.[54]

When the Lane Rebels arrived in the fall of 1835, their power was complete. The school's catalogue for that fall listed a faculty of seven, three of whom had come to Oberlin with the "rebels" and only one of whom had been a part of the three member faculty the year before.[55] The new arrivals had essentially "refounded the institution when it was on the verge of collapse."[56] While there were other students in the collegiate department, the seminarians were clearly the leaders. And the arrival of Charles Finney, the nation's best known revivalist, gave the school prestige and would influence its orientation for the next several decades.[57]

One place where Shipherd and the new arrivals were in complete agreement was on the importance of manual labor. Before the Lane rebellion, Shipherd had insisted, "The Manual Labor Department will receive unusual attention, being not (as is too common), regarded as an unimportant appendage to the literary department; but systematized and incorporated with it....All will be required to labor...."[58] For a student body, many of whom were coming to Oberlin by way of Lane and Oneida, this requirement could not be more acceptable.

After the somewhat accidental invention of the manual labor

system by Gale, it quickly became popular in a number of schools. But in the 1830s no school would rival Oberlin in its complete allegiance to the importance of manual labor as a part of a collegiate and theological curriculum. The school circular of 1834 noted that first of all the manual labor department was indispensable to preserving the students' health.[59] The second goal of the department was to promote clear and strong thought, together with a happy moral temperament, "there being an intimate sympathy between soul and body." And the third desirable effect was to help pay the costs of education.[60] In later generations, the opportunity to pay a large part of the cost of education often became the prime advantage of manual labor.[61] But for Oberlin's first student generation the moral benefits, especially as those moral benefits came to be linked with other symbols of the anti-slavery cause, were primary.

Although he was to be the dominant figure at Oberlin for the next forty years, Charles Finney was reluctant to make the move.[62] He had refused a Tappan offer to join the students in Cincinnati, but it was difficult to refuse a plea from the rebels when they wrote in January, 1835:

> We need more practical preaching power—more knowledge of revival measures than we can obtain at any Seminary at the West—and perhaps in the country. We must inhale another theological atmosphere. It would be the delight of our hearts to complete our education under the guidance of one whose intellectual and moral contact would, as we believe, give us an onward momentum....[63]

Finally, Finney agreed to move to Oberlin when all his demands for his own academic freedom and the rights of Black students had been met, along with a generous promise of Tappan support.[64] Still, he arranged to spend only half of every year at Oberlin, noting that his New York City congregation, "consents to let me go to Oberlin on the condition that I be at liberty to spend 3 or 4 months in the winter of each year in this city."[65]

Throughout his long Oberlin career, Finney continued to be often on the move, leading revivals, attending conventions, meeting other obligations. Finney was always primarily a roving evangelist for his version of the gospel. Teaching theology was always secondary. When he was on campus, Finney reached the most students through his preaching in the college chapel. Here students in all parts of the institution could learn both his theology and his style of ministry.[66] But for those in the theology department, there was more.

Finney taught both the classes in systematic theology and pastoral theology. In the former, he expounded his increasingly strong beliefs in the possibility of perfection and in the need for preachers to actively call people not only to repentance, but to perfect obedience and "sanctification."[67] While Finney often left the details vague, in the hands of Weld and other students, this doctrine would be most useful in calling the nation to repent of the sin of slavery and actively change its ways in relation to that sin.[68]

It was in the pastoral theology courses, however, where Finney most clearly outlined his ideal of the proper minister for his generation. In the course of his lectures, Finney gave a wide range of advice, and painted a picture of what he expected of those who would carry his message. Naturally, first and foremost, was "A living, ardent piety—not last years piety—but living now."[69] Equally important, this piety had to be made known to others effectively. The key, of course, he told his students was that, "You must know God. You must know the power of prayer or you cannot describe it."[70] And beyond that, the congregation had to be respected. "Men are not cabbage heads," he warned. "You have God as one of your hearers."[71]

A large part of the course was devoted to very personal concerns. Many of Finney's students, especially in the later years, had grown up on the frontier. While pious, a minister also had to be careful of the impressions being made. "If he be a man of ill manners, it will destroy his influence."[72]

The minister was not merely to make a good impression, however. Finney also wanted him to be actively involved in winning souls and perfecting individuals and the world. As he insisted, "The minister must be willing to carry out every branch of reform."[73] For Finney the primary means of such work was always to be preaching, calling individuals to repentance. But there was more. He urged ministers to be leaders in their community and insisted that, "He is not to admit for a moment that he is going out of his sphere,"[74] when taking a secular role as a reform leader.[75] "The church," Finney warned, "has in many cases been made to think that religion consists in feelings"[76] For Finney, action was the test of feelings. And this meant political action, for it was in the political sphere that many of the issues of the day—especially slavery—would be settled. Of course, some "will go so far that they run into fanaticism." But this did not excuse the rest from involvement.[77]

Finney taught the course in pastoral theology at Oberlin from 1835 to 1875, encouraging generations of midwestern ministers to preach a gospel which was both individualistic and activist in its call for repentance and a new life, first for individuals, but also for the society in which they found themselves.[78] This "Oberlin perfectionism" and the model of ministry associated with it made "the hand of Oberlin"[79] something to be feared not only by old time antagonists like Lyman Beecher, but by the majority of those in the major denominations, activist or not.

Oberlin reciprocated the distrust. One visitor compared the mood at commencement at Western Reserve College in nearby Hudson, Ohio with that of Oberlin:

> At Hudson they manifested great reverence for the church
> and her institutions as they now exist; at Oberlin the church
> was often criminated. At Hudson we had the bright side of
> the picture—all was well; at Oberlin this was pronounced a
> 'degenerate age,' 'a faithless generation,' and 'reform' was
> demanded.[80]

Among the church colleges of the frontier, there was probably no other where the church would be "criminated." But Oberlin's religion was different. For all the differences in their work, both Finney and Weld called people to be actively involved in saving souls and changing nations. Institutions, church institutions or others, were much less important, and indeed if not a help to the cause at hand, it was appropriate to label them the hindrances which they were.

Having led the Lane Rebels through their departure from one school and through their year of exile, Theodore Weld did not accompany them to Oberlin. The exile year in Cincinnati was the end of his formal theological schooling. For the rest of his life he continued his own unique ministry as an anti-slavery organizer and activist.[81]

In fact, Weld had been the first one offered the theological professorship at Oberlin, but had vigorously argued that Finney should play that role while he continued the anti-slavery organizing which was his primary vocation.[82] One of his first moves in his new position as agent for the American Anti-Slavery Society, however, took Weld back to Ohio. He needed agents to carry on the anti-slavery campaign in that state, and the natural place to turn was to his old allies. In August, 1835, thirteen of the Lane Rebels met with Weld in Cleveland for two weeks and then scattered throughout the state as agents for anti-slavery.[83] The pattern would be repeated as Weld became a virtual one-man employment agency for the anti-slavery cause.

In May, 1836, just as many of the original Lane Rebels were finishing their theological course, the American Anti-Slavery Society adopted a new campaign to evangelize the nation for abolitionism. The pamphlet campaigns of the last few years had not worked well. Written materials were too easy to destroy or ignore. What was needed were revivalists. Turning to biblical precedent, they voted to send out a mission of the seventy to convert the land. Funds would be raised to send out this number to preach the sin of slavery and the need for the repentance of abolitionism. Weld was commissioned to choose the agents.[84]

Again he turned to his old classmates, especially now that many of them were just on the point of seeking their first ministerial appointments. Again he traveled to Ohio to recruit. Eventually thirty of the fifty-four students who had signed the students' statement at Lane became a part of the cause.[85] Some stayed for a few years and then moved on to other forms of ministry. Others spent their lives in the anti-slavery movement. But among them they carried the mix of revivalism and activism which had emerged from Oberlin to all of the free states of the union. Weld's biographer has correctly described their form of ministry, "Rather than agents, the Lane rebels were evangelists of abolitionism, and their power to move communities was one with the power of Finney."[86] It was also a kind of evangelism not seen previously on the American stage.

Historians have continued to argue over the importance of the Finney-Weld-Tappan strain of abolitionism in comparison with that of Frederick Douglas and William Lloyd Garrison or the more narrowly economic concerns of other northerners who also opposed slavery.[87] Even among these evangelical abolitionists, there were also differences. At times Finney worried that Tappan and Weld would raise so much hostility by their activity that the cause of revivals would be damaged. Thus he wrote to Tappan:

> I feel so anxious about the movement of the Abolitionists just at the present state of the question, that every thing should be conducted wisely, that I feel constrained before I leave New York to drop a few suggestions to you upon paper.[88]

Whatever the constraints that Finney wished for, he was seldom successful in slowing Weld or the Tappans. And his own commitment to perfectionism, linked with his lack of concern for the institutional church freed him from many of the worries faced by a Lyman Beecher.

In addition to their importance in the crusade which led to emancipation, both Weld and Finney also played another role. They were creating a new form of ministry for American Protestantism. In his own day Lyman Beecher had helped to define the activist minister as one who used the pastorate as a base for involvement in a wide range of activities designed to reform and Christianize the nation. Finney had taken activism a step further. For him the needs of the day demanded that some ministers give up the settled pastorate in one place and move on as evangelists from place to place preaching immediate repentance and regeneration. Evangelists were to "win souls to Christ and gather a flock," while pastors were to "feed, lead, superintend and watch over it."[89]

Weld had learned from both. But he also moved beyond them. In his career as student rebel, evangelist, and anti-slavery agent, Weld developed a new definition of the activist minister. For Weld, the activist minister was a preacher, evangelist, and organizer for a cause. Few parishes would have considered such a radical. But neither the parish nor the revival meeting served as his base. Rather his support came from a group of people committed to a single cause. And as agent of that cause, Weld defined his own form of ministry. It was the beginning of a new, often powerful, if always minority understanding of the ministry for the American churches.

FOOTNOTES

[1] H.B. Stanton and George Whipple to Charles G. Finney, Cumminville, Ohio, January 10, 1835, Document #1151, Finney papers, Oberlin College Archives, Oberlin Ohio.

[2] "A Statement of the Reasons Which Induced the Students of Lane Seminary to Dissolve Their Connection With That Institution," December 15, 1834 (Cincinnati: 1834).

[3] In this analysis and subsequent parts of this chapter, I have drawn heavily on my earlier work, *Pedagogue for God's Kingdom: Lyman Beecher and the Second Great Awakening* (Lanham, MD: University Press of America, 1985); There have been many other interpretations of the Lane debates. Lawrence Thomas Lesick, *The Lane Rebels: Evangelicalism and Antislavery in Antebellum America* (Metuchen, NJ: The Scarecrow Press, Inc., 1980) is an exhaustive study of the topic focusing especially on the relationship of evangelical theology and antislavery. For excellent earlier studies see also, Robert Samuel Fletcher, *A History of Oberlin College*, 2 vols. (Oberlin: 1943), Vol. I, pp. 150-166; Gilbert H. Barnes, *The Antislavery Impulse, 1830-1844* (New York: 1933, 1964), pp. 64-73; Vincent Harding, "Lyman Beecher and the Transformation of American Protestantism, 1775-1863," unpublished Ph.D. dissertation, University of Chicago, 1965, pp. 460-505; and Malcolm Warford, "The Lane Student Rebellion," unpublished paper presented at Teachers College, Columbia University, spring 1971.

[4] "Copy of a Letter on the Subject of a Theological Seminary in the West, (Circular), J. L. Wilson to Rev. and Dear Sir, Cincinnati, September, 1822," in William Warren Sweet, *Religion on the American Frontier, Vol. II, The Presbyterians 1783-1840* (New York: 1936), pp. 590-91.

[5] Harriet Beecher Stowe quoted in Lyman Beecher, *Autobiography*, 2 vols. (New York: 1864, edited by Barbara Cross, Cambridge, MA: 1961), Vol. II, p. 218.

[6] See for example, G. H. Maxwell, "History of the Synod of Cincinnati," handwritten document, Presbyterian Historical Society, Philadelphia, Pennsylvania; Maurice W. Armstrong, Lefferts A. Loetscher, and Charles A. Anderson, *The Presbyterian Enterprise: Sources of American Presbyterian History* (Philadelphia: 1956) provides a more up to date review of the issues involved in the old school-new school split within the Presbyterian church in the 1830s.

[7] While the primary focus of this paper is on differing understandings of the role of the minister among activists—that is between Beecher, Finney, and Weld—the same questions regarding differing understandings of the nature of the ministry could profitably be applied to the whole old school-new school

72

split within the Presbyterian church.

[8] "Lyman Beecher to Ebenezer Porter, Boston, June, 1829," in Beecher, *Autobiography*, Vol. II, p. 139.

[9] Harriet Beecher Stowe in Beecher, *Autobiography*, Vol. II, p. 86.

[10] "Ebenezer Porter to Lyman Beecher, May 22, 1829," in Beecher, *Autobiography*, Vol. II, p. 120.

[11] For more on Beecher's early ministry see Beecher, *Autobiography*, Vol. I; and also my *Pedagogue for God's Kingdom*, pp. 14-21; and Charles I Foster, *An Errand of Mercy: The Evangelical United Front, 1790-1837*, (Chapel Hill: 1960).

[12] "L.B. to Catharine, Boston, July 8, 1830," in Beecher, *Autobiography*, Vol. II, p. 167.

[13] "L.B. to Mr. Cornelius, February 25, 1815," in Beecher, *Autobiography*, Vol. I, p. 211.

[14] "L.B. to Catharine, Boston, July 8, 1830," in Beecher, *Autobiography*, Vol. I, p. 167.

[15] "L.B. to E. Cornelius, February 25, 1815," in *Autobiography*, Vol. I, p. 211.

[16] Beecher, *Autobiography*, Vol. I, p. 45.

[17] "LB to Trustees of Lane Seminary, March 17, 1832," Beecher, *Autobiography*, Vol. II, p. 190.

[18] Beecher, *Autobiography*, Vol. II, p. 222.

[19] D. Howe Allen, *The Life and Services of Rev. Lyman Beecher, D.D., A Commemorative Discourse* (Cincinnati: 1863) p. 22.

[20] Beecher, *Autobiography*, Vol. II, p. 244.

[21] Charles G. Finney, *Memoirs* (New York: 1876), p. 24.

[22] Beecher, *Autobiography*, Vol. II, pp. 66-80.

[23] Douglas M. Sloan, "Harmony, Chaos, and Consensus: The American College Curriculum," in *Teachers College Record*, Vol. 73, No. 2 (December, 1971), p. 231.

[24] Finney, *Memoirs*, pp. 45-46.

[25] ibid, p. 56.

[26] George Washington Gale, *Autobiography* (New York: 1964), p. 276.

[27] For more on the history of Oneida Institute, in addition to Gale's *Autobiography*, see Fletcher, Vol. I, pp. 34-43; Dana Bigelow, "Whitestown Seminary," (Utica, N.Y.: n.d.); and Gilbert H. Barnes and Dwight L. Dumond, eds., *Letters of Theodore Dwight Weld, Angelina Grimke Weld, and Sarah Grimke, 1822-1844*, 2 vols. (New York: 1934), p. 17, "editors note."

[28] "Introduction," in *Weld-Grimke*, Vol. I, p. xxi.

[29] ibid, Vol. I, pp. xx-xxii.

[30] Bertram Wyatt-Brown, *Lewis Tappan and the Evangelical War Against Slavery* (Cleveland: 1969), p. 122.

[31] Barnes, p. 41.

[32] "F. Y. Vail to T. D. Weld, November, 1831," in *Weld-Grimke*, Vol. I, pp. 58-

[33] "Calvin Waterbury to Weld, August 3, 1832," in *Weld-Grimke*, Vol. I, p. 82.

[34] "H.B. Stanton, E. Weed, S.W. Starter and C. Waterbury to Weld, Lane Seminary (Cincinnati, Ohio) August 2, 1832," in *Weld-Grimke*, Vol. I, p. 79.

[35] "F.Y. Vail to Weld, November, 1831," in *Weld-Grimke*, Vol. I, p. 59.

[36] cited in Beecher, *Autobiography*, Vol. II, p. 212.

[37] For a brief review of Beecher's fight with the old school Presbyterians see my *Pedagogue for God's Kingdom*, pp. 124-127. A very detailed account is contained in Trial and Acquittal of Lyman Beecher, D.D. before the Presbytery of Cincinnati, on charges preferred by Joshua L. Wilson, D.D. Reported for the New York Observer, by Mr. Stansbury of Washington, D.C. (Cincinnati: 1835).

[38] "Weld to Arthur Tappan, Joshua Leavitt, and Elizur Wright, Jr., Lane Seminary, Walnut Hills, Ohio, November 22, 1833," in *Weld-Grimke*, Vol, I, p. 120; for a biased but useful account of Weld's importance for the anti-slavery movement in America, see Barnes, *The AntiSlavery Impulse*.

[39] Wyatt-Brown, pp. 121-122.

[40] See for example, J. Earl Thompson, Jr., "Lyman Beecher's Long Road to Conservative Abolitionism," *Church History*, Vol. 42 (March, 1973), p. 98.

[41] There are many descriptions of the "Lane Debates." See, for example, Fletcher, Vol. I, pp. 150-166; Barnes, pp. 64-73; and Harding, pp. 460-505. While interpretation and details differ, the general outline is clear.

[42] "Weld to Lewis Tappan, Lane Seminary (Cincinnati, Ohio), March 18, 1834," in *Weld-Grimke*, Vol. I, p. 133.

[43] See, for example, "Weld to James Hall, Editor of the *Western Monthly Magazine*, May, 1834," in *Weld-Grimke*, Vol. I, pp. 136-146.

[44] See Beecher, *Autobiography*, Vol. II, p. 244.

[45] "Lewis Tappan to T. Weld, September 29, 1834," Slavery MSS, Box II, New York Historical Society," cited in Wyatt-Brown, p. 128.

[46] Beecher, *Autobiography*, Vol. II, p. 246

[47] Beecher, *Autobiography*, Vol. II, p. 245.

[48] Beecher, *Autobiography*, Vol. II, pp. 247-248; Fletcher, pp. 161-162.

[49] "A Statement of the Reasons Which Induced the Students of Lane Seminary to Dissolve Their Connection with that Institution," December 15, 1834 (Cincinnati: 1834).

[50] There are several accounts of the "Lane Rebels" course after leaving Lane. Among the more useful are Wyatt-Brown, pp. 126ff.; Barnes, pp. 74ff.; and Finney, *Memoirs*, pp. 332-335.

[51] By far the best history of Oberlin is Fletcher; also useful is James H. Fairchild, *Oberlin: The Colony and the College*, 1833-1883 (Oberlin: 1883).

[52] *The First Annual Report of the Oberlin Collegiate Institute* (Elyria, Ohio: November, 1834), p. 5.

[53] Wyatt-Brown, pp. 128-129; see also Fletcher.

[54] Finney, *Memoirs*, pp. 332-333; Barnes, pp. 75-77.

[55] See *The First Annual Report of the Oberlin Collegiate Institute* (Elyria, Ohio, November, 1834), p. 4; and the *Catalogue of the Trustees, Officers, and Students of the Oberlin Collegiate Institute Together with the Second Annual Report* (Cleveland: 1835), p. 5. The one faculty carry over was James Dascomb, Professor of Chemistry, Botany and Physiology.

[56] Fletcher, Vol. II, p. 726.

[57] "An Appeal to the Philanthropists of Great Britain on Behalf of Oberlin College—by Theodore and Angelina Weld," in *Weld-Grimke*, pp. 741-744.

[58] *Ohio Atlas and Elyria Advertiser*, October 17, 1833, cited in Fletcher, Vol. II, p. 634.

[59] *The First Annual Report of the Oberlin Collegiate Institute* (Elyria, Ohio: November, 1834), p. 6.

[60] ibid.

[61] Fletcher, Vol. II, p. 511.

[62] Finney, *Memoirs*, pp. 332-333.

[63] "H.B. Stanton and George Whipple to C. G. Finney, Cumminsville, January 10, 1835," Document #1151, Finney papers, Oberlin College Archives, Oberlin, Ohio.

[64] Finney, *Memoirs*, pp. 333-335.

[65] "C. G. Finney to H. B. Stanton and George Whipple", New York, January 18, 1835," Document #1153, Finney papers, Oberlin College Archives, Oberlin, Ohio.

[66] Fletcher, Vol. II, p. 576, 688, and 889-893; Fletcher correctly summarized Finney's role at Oberlin in stating that while he was in many ways a figurehead, "he was a very impressive figurehead." (Vol. II, p. 893).

[67] Fairchild, pp. 90-91.

[68] Barnes, pp. 100-108.

[69] William A. Westervelt, Pastoral Theology lecture notes, handwritten MSS, file 30/120, Oberlin College Archives, Oberlin, Ohio, p. 3. Oberlin records show that Westervelt was a student in the Theology Department 1843-1846. These notes were most likely taken during his senior year, 1845-46.

[70] E. J. Comings, "Oberlin, July, 1837, Prof. Finney's Lectures on Pastoral Theology," typed mss. in the Robert Fletcher papers, Oberlin College Archives, Oberlin, Ohio, p. 3.

[71] Westervelt, p. 13.

[72] Westervelt, p. 3.

[73] Westervelt, p. 2.

[74] Westervelt, p. 3.

[75] Westervelt, p. 2.

[76] Westervelt, p. 2.

[77] All above are from Westervelt, p. 2.

[78] Fletcher, Vol. II, p. 899. Fletcher's study represents a careful review of

Finney's lectures both from his own notes and those of several students available in the Oberlin Archives.

[79] Lyman Beecher to Lydia Beecher, Columbus, (Ohio), February 23, 1839, Beecher papers, Stowe-Day Library, Hartford, CT.

[80] Fletcher, Vol. II, p. 835.

[81] Barnes, p. 76.

[82] ibid.

[83] ibid.

[84] Barnes, p. 104.

[85] Barnes, p. 77.

[86] Barnes, p. 78.

[87] William G. McLoughlin, "Introduction to the Harbinger Edition," in Barnes, pp. vii-xxxi.

[88] C.G. Finney to Dear Bro. Tappan [Arthur], New York, April 30, 1836, Document #1215, Finney papers, Oberlin College Archives, Oberlin, Ohio.

[89] Fletcher, Vol. II, p. 728.

PART II

EXPERIENCE AND EDUCATION

THEOLOGICAL EDUCATION
IN THE NEW AMERICAN DENOMINATIONS

Chapter IV
WHAT WOULD HAVE BECOME
OF THE MASSES OF THE PEOPLE?

THE DEVELOPMENT OF NEW PATTERNS
FOR THE TRAINING OF REVIVAL PREACHERS

In a retrospective sermon late in his life, John A. Broadus, one of the leaders of the movement to found seminaries among the southern Baptists, reviewed the variety of options in preparing for ministry which were available in the nineteenth century and asked:

> I have profound respect for the ministry of the Presbyterian and Episcopal brethren....But if it hadn't been for the great Methodist and great Baptist bodies, and some others like them, who have encouraged men to preach that were destitute of this artificial course of training, what in the world would have become of the masses of the people?[1]

It was an important question, what would have become of the masses of the Protestants in the United States if a classical education had been required for all future ministers? Indeed by the early years of the nineteenth century, the need to find an answer to this question had reached crisis proportions among Protestants in many parts of the United States.

For Baptists like Broadus, as well as the majority of Methodists and those who left the Presbyterian Church to found the Disciples of Christ and the Cumberland Presbyterians, there were at least two problems with the traditional ordination requirements of the reformed denominations including the Presbyterians and the Congregationalists. The first problem was most obvious. There simply weren't enough classically trained ministers to go around, and the need was pressing. But in addition to this problem many had come to believe, as Charles Finney told his Presbytery in 1822 while refusing their offer of support in seminary, "I plainly told them that I would not put myself under such an influence as they had been under; that I was confident they had been wrongly educated ...."[2] A classical education was not only hard to get. In many parts of the growing nation it seemed to cut a minister off from the direct contact with his audience—from an essential kind of experience—which was needed for success as a preacher. Given these concerns with the traditional ways of educating ministers, new ways had to be found. And among the majority of Methodists and Baptists, and those who left the Presbyterian church, new and innovative ways of theological education were developed in the years between the American Revolution and the Civil War.

The eighteenth century, of course, had also witnessed a wide range in forms of theological education. But amidst that diversity there had been certain agreements across the denominational spectrum about the importance of certain standards, usually symbolized by a college degree or equivalent learning demonstrated through examinations. Yet what happened when the people were there, and the preachers were there, but the preachers did not have a classical training and were not sure they wanted it?

The historians of the Cumberland Presbyterians describe the answer their predecessors gave to the question:

> People who had participated in the camp meetings went home enthusiastic to spread the good news. As a result of the rapid growth in the number of churches, the need for more ordained ministers was keenly felt. Not more than one-third of the churches had regular preaching services; consequently, Transylvania Presbytery, at its meeting in October 1801, at the Muddy River Church, licensed four men...as exhorters and catechizers.... following the example of the early church in Scotland ...that gifted young men be chosen from the laity and licensed to exhort, even though they lacked a classical education.[3]

Within a decade this action would lead to the expulsion of Cumberland Presbytery from the Presbyterian church, and the formation of a new denomination committed to the spread of the revival even if the result was the ordination of preachers who did not know their classics.

Questions about educational requirements were always especially disturbing on the frontier where there were never enough college or seminary trained candidates but there were preachers arising out of the revivals claiming the call of the Spirit. Sectional tension and jealousy tended to aggravate the issue. A fair number of westerners did not trust the sort of schooling going on in the "east" because it tended to elevate the clergy beyond the common people and, even worse, make them dependent on their books and written sermons rather than the movement of the Spirit which was central to the revival experience.

Charles Finney was not the only one who was wary of the results of certain kinds of schooling. Alexander Campbell wrote sarcastically of the ministerial candidate who...

> reads volumes of scholastic divinity, and obtains, from sermon books and skeletons of sermons, models for future practice. Bodies of divinity adapted to the sect to whom he looks for maintenance, are closely studied; and the bible is sometimes referred to as a book of proofs for the numerous articles of his creed....A clergyman thus qualified can deliver a very popular and orthodox sermon without any grace; as easily too as a lawyer can plead the cause of his client without grace.[4]

Campbell was not opposed to schools. Later he became a college president, and developed an array of informal training programs for ministers. Yet he feared any schooling which made one independent of the Spirit or which isolated ministers from the people. Therefore he insisted, "ministerial education should be given in connection with the colleges and not in isolated seminaries specifically for that purpose."[5]

American religion in this post-revolutionary generation was experiencing the same tensions as American political life. And those who struggled for a new form of theological education had

81

their counterparts in the emerging Jacksonian movement. Indeed, it is only by understanding the popularity of Andrew Jackson as a political figure and the movement which transformed American political life forever and led to his election as the nation's seventh president, that one can understand the developments in the field of theological education—and in the understanding of the nature of the ministry—among many of the same people who would be politically drawn to Jackson.

John William Ward, in his thoughtful study, *Andrew Jackson: Symbol for an Age*, described the changes in American life which led Jackson to so dominate it in the years between 1812 and his death in 1845. In Jacksonian America, Ward argued, the democratic leader, "faces a delicate task. He must lead men and still be one of them. According to a naive democratic philosophy of equality, the vertical distance that separates the leader from the led must be denied."[6] Almost exactly the same issue applied to preachers as political leaders in many parts of the nation.

Given these developments, the proper training for ministers, as for political and military leaders, suddenly changed dramatically. Thus after his famous victory in the Battle of New Orleans, Andrew Jackson addressed his troops. "Reasoning always from false principles," Jackson insisted, "[the British] expected little opposition from men whose officers even were not in uniform, who were ignorant of the rules of dress, and who had never been caned into discipline. Fatal mistake!"[7] The actual mistakes of the British were considerably more complicated than popular opinion—or Jackson's speeches—implied. But it was Jackson who correctly gauged—and came to symbolize—the temper of the new nation's spirit in the first third of the nineteenth century.

One of Jackson's officers at New Orleans described:

'those modest and simple sons of nature': Instinctively valiant, disciplined without having passed through the formal training of reviews and garrison manoeuvres, they evinced [attributes] which were of far more avail than scientific tactics.'[8]

As Ward noted, "The rejection of formalism and training here is based on the assumption that there is a superior strength that is spontaneous." Again and again, the speeches after New Orleans stressed the same theme. Training in formal military tactics could never stand up to the natural, spontaneous skills which were, "far more formidable than the practised skill and discipline of regulars."[9]

It was in this same spirit that the General Conference of the Methodist Episcopal Church, South, resolved in 1854,

> That we earnestly recommend to all the Colleges under the care of our Church, not to establish any department for the exclusive education of the Ministry, or those who are preparing for the Ministry.[10]

The great danger, proclaimed again and again in Methodist literature was that exclusive education for those preparing for the ministry in any setting separated from the rest of the population, was that they would lose their spontaneous dependence on the Holy Spirit; the same spontaneity which had given Jackson's sharp shooters such accuracy in New Orleans. The proper way, the Methodists asserted, to "elevate also the intellectual character of our preaching" would be to "educate the masses."[11] The revivalists would not permit the rise of any elite out of touch with the spirit of the times or with the common people. The image of the minister as learned gentleman, part of a learned, as well as pious, elite, was gone.

Out of these concerns emerged an amazing variety of forms of theological study. Probably few aspiring ministers actually kept up with the Methodist injunction: "From six in the morning till twelve (allowing an hour for breakfast,) read, with much prayer, some of our best religious tracts."[12] But in their own churches, in two week "preacher's institutes" and four year courses of study, in the apprenticeship of riding the circuit with an experienced preacher, and in attending academies and colleges, the ministers of the newer denominations developed new approaches to theological education. It was a theological education more in keeping with an understanding of the ministry which was growing in the new nation. In the newer denominations, the minister had been transformed from learned gentleman to a Jacksonian democrat, a spontaneous, although inspired, man of the people.

For those who distrusted formal preparation for the ministry, the primary agency of education was often the local congregation. In addition to Sunday school or other forms of instruction, there was also the more subtle, but probably more significant influence for many a promising youth of watching the preacher at work, gaining an impression of the role, and having the opportunity to try it out in some small ministerial tasks in the home church.

After a time such a youth might graduate to the position of an assistant to the minister. From there it was only a small step to a pastorate or preaching circuit of one's own. Of course, long before the age of Jackson, beginning one's preparation for ministry at one's home church had been the pattern for many. What was new in the early nineteenth century was the way in which apprenticeship gradually became the central or terminal experience in education for many candidates, and thus assumed far greater importance in the larger economy of theological education. Such a move was a reform almost undreamed of in the eighteenth century.

The experience of the Sandy Creek Separate Baptist Church in Randolph County, North Carolina, represents one example of this kind of parish based theological education. The church was founded by Shubal Stearns who immigrated to North Carolina from New England in 1755. The initial congregation consisted of approximately a dozen members including one Daniel Marshall. Soon Marshall became one of Stearns' assistants. G. W. Paschal describes the growth of the congregation:

> The preaching of Stearns and his assistants resulted in the
> establishment of a station at Abbot's Creek, 30 miles away,
> in less than a year. It soon became an independent church
> with Marshall as pastor, probably in 1756. In three years,
> when a station at Deep Creek became independent, the total
> membership of the three churches was 900.[13]

New Separate Baptist churches continued to branch out from the Sandy Creek congregation. "In 17 years 42 churches had been formed and 125 ministers, many of them ordained, had joined the movement."[14] Such growth from a single church was, of course, remarkable. But the pattern was not. In settling a new country, it made good sense for one church to spawn others who in turn had their own descendents. And it made equal sense for those who achieved leadership and became assistants in the parent church to use their training as ministers of the new churches.

It was a pattern which fit well with the understanding of the nature of the ministry in Jacksonian America. In any case, no other ministers were available. But even if more formally trained ministers had been available, they might well have been less effective in a rapidly growing movement, such as the Separate Baptists. The church itself was the place of worship, the agent of mission, and the location of theological education. The curriculum may have been limited, and practical, but the testing was rigorous enough. If one became proficient enough in revival preaching to help a new church gather, one was proficient enough to tend the flock.

Preacher's Institutes

In an 1835 issue of the *Millennial Harbinger*, the more or less official journal of the Disciples of Christ, Alexander Campbell announced the launching of a new educational enterprise, a "School of the Preachers":

> It was agreed by all those who labor in the word and teaching, present at the annual meeting in Newburg, Ohio, to have stated meetings for their own edification in the matter and manner of public instruction in the christian religion. All the brethren are sensible that they have not attained the highest degree of excellence in the manner of contending for the faith formerly delivered to the saints; and even the matter of their public discourse is not, themselves being judges, always what it ought to be. At present there is no means of improvement but in the slow and gradual development of the school of experience....[15]

The proposed meeting, Campbell explained, would be an opportunity for all Disciples preachers in the area to spend a week together. Each one would preach a sermon; and "these discourses shall then be examined freely as to matter and manner, in committee of the whole, preaching and teaching brethren alone."[16] In addition the "school" would ponder some subject such as the best principles of interpreting Scriptures. If nothing else, these occasions provided an opportunity for fellowship and group support among ministers spread over a lonely frontier area.

Campbell had devised an institution well-adapted to the needs of his preachers. Many of them had experienced all of their initial theological education in their home church and in revivals. College education, while perhaps desirable, was hardly practical for this group of first generation Disciples preachers, many of whom supported themselves through employment other than their preaching.

The "School for Preachers" was something different, however. It was possible to get away for a week, and it was hardly enough time to weaken one's ties to the rest of the population or one's spontaneity. Yet a week of discussion, mutual criticism, and some presentations by an expert like Campbell, could make quite a difference in the work of a preacher. That indeed was Campbell's conviction when he reported on the experience three months later:

> It was unanimously agreed by all the brethren present that the meeting was of the most profitable character; that much information was elicited, many inadvertencies and improprieties corrected; and every one seemed to return home determined to be more vigilant, more studious, more circumspect, and more scriptural in thought and expression than before.[17]

Fourteen Disciples ministers from Ohio had participated in this first school, and they had agreed to continue the experiment.

These meetings became a regular quarterly event wherever there was a sufficient number of Disciples preachers. It was generally agreed that these gatherings should be for the preachers only, or at least the part in which sermons were criticized— although the preaching time could be an occasion for a revival. Criticisms before the public were considered "incalculably injurious," exciting in the subject of criticism "a disposition to apologize away his reproof, or to justify himself, sometimes unqualifiedly."[18]

After the Civil War another version of the schools for preachers emerged—free lectures over a two-month period for ministers at the Disciples' colleges. One such course was described in the following way:

> These Lectures are designed especially for such preachers of the Gospel as cannot take the regular course of the Biblical Institute. They will be popular in style, and arranged to cover all the most practical wants of the Preacher, in Sacred History, Biblical Literature, Church History, Christology and Homiletics.[19]

But none of these courses, though often demanding, were considered to be a proper "substitute for a regular College or University course."[20] By the close of the Civil War, a college education had come to be an ideal, if not always an expected reality among Disciples preachers. They still distrusted separate seminaries. And they still made provision for those who could not attend college. Yet, signs of change were in the air.

In the Civil War era the institute form of theological education also became popular in other denominations. A group of Illinois Baptists declared in 1863 that:

> ...our own sense of the need of constant improvement and increase of knowledge in our Master's work, and our observation of the wants of the ministry throughout the State, convinces us that we ought to secure additional means of instruction, not merely for those preparing for the ministry, but for those who are the actual pastors and ministers of our State. We believe that this very important object can be most effectually and economically secured by a Ministers' Institute, to be held annually for one or two weeks at one or two points in the State, where as many as possible of our ministers may assemble and place themselves under thorough and practical instruction by the best ministerial educators of our land.[21]

The institutes began the following year with eighty people attending a program at the old University of Chicago. Within two years, and the close of the war, 180 were attending these annual programs. By this time, the Baptists (like the Disciples) had moved away from "mutual improvement" to the use of experts in a short-term college experience. And like the Disciples, the Baptists of Illinois warned that these institutes were no substitute for college.[22] Yet for many ministers of many denominations various forms of preachers' institutes, whether in the earlier form of mutual improvement or the later one of specialized instruction, represented a reform in theological education and a major improvement over their previous training.

Circuit Riding the the Course of Study

In 1856, when he was an old man, Peter Cartwright set out to tell the story of his life as an itinerant Methodist preacher on the Mississippi Valley frontier. Converted and called to the ministry at age seventeen, with little formal education, Cartwright became one of the best known symbols of Methodism in the new nation, the itinerant circuit rider who abandoned a settled life for the horse-back ride through the wilderness with a charge to "preach in the morning, where he can get hearers."[23] Throughout his *Autobiography* Cartwright made quite clear his opinion of other denominations and of their theological seminaries which had been developing in these years:

> The Presbyterians, and other Calvinistic branches of the Protestant Church, used to contend for an educated ministry, for pews, for instrumental music, for a congregational or stated salaried minister. The Methodists universally opposed these ideas; and the illiterate Methodist preachers actually set the world on fire, (the American world at least,) while they were lighting their matches![24]

For Cartwright, the theological seminary and the settled parish minister were intrinsically connected institutions imported from Congregationalism. He opposed both.

Cartwright's opposition to seminaries was not based on any anti-intellectual tendencies. He simply saw no need to change the circuit riding system since it provided Methodism with a means of both theological education and ministry. Many of the earliest ministers in the Wesleyan movement had been imported from England, where some had trained with Wesley himself. Once on the American continent, however, they adopted a system of their own, first devised by the organizing genius of American Methodism, Francis Asbury.

All ministers in this system were itinerants. Local preachers or those who were forced through age and ill health to remain in one place were not considered ministers in "full connection." The itinerants traveled through a circuit marked out at the annual conference and assigned to a rider. The circuit rider was supervised by a senior or presiding elder who traveled over an even larger area and supervised several circuits. Finally, there were the bishops such as Asbury who traveled the whole nation. The success of this system in building one of the nation's largest denominations is well-known. Yet, few latter-day scholars have examined it as a method of theological education, which it assuredly was. Among its other features, the circuit provided an easy means of learning by apprenticeship. So, for instance, William Henry Milburn remembered his education:

> As I went the round of the district, with my venerable guide, philosopher, and friend, riding sometimes for whole days through almost limitless stretches of prairie, much time was spent in asking and answering questions concerning theology and kindred sciences, in which he was profoundly versed. His full and satisfactory explanations in response to my eager queries, together with his exhaustive discourses delivered in public, afforded me a large store of material to digest and assimilate.[25]

In Milburn's case he was able not only to discuss theology, but to watch the preacher and quiz him on his work. In time, he did some of the preaching and was duly corrected and criticized by his "venerable guide." Milburn also remembered the "strong bonds" which were created, simply through the experience of the shared loneliness, besides the shared education. According to another pleased observer, the circuit

> ...furnished the young preachers with an apprenticeship that
> was invaluable, the equivalent of which no ordinary school
> can provide. It assured them the practical, personal over-
> sight of senior preachers in the actual work of the ministry;
> the stimulus and profit of contact with superior minds; the
> advantages of living models; and the blessed contagion of
> maturer character.[26]

Although the speaker was viewing the system at a time when it
was fading and may have tended to romanticize, he managed to
capture its essence.

Meanwhile the Cumberland Presbyterians referred to their
circuit system as the "saddlebags school" for young preachers.
Silas Newton Davis, who would become one of the better known
Cumberland preachers, was converted, and believed himself
called to preach at age seventeen. Despite Davis' limited schooling, B. H. Pierson decided to

> take him with me on the circuit, and teach him, as I might
> have opportunity, English Grammar and other things that I
> deemed important, and that, on becoming a candidate for
> the ministry, I knew the Presbytery would require him to
> know.[27]

The Presbytery, in fact, required an additional summer term at
an academy, after which it proceeded to license and ordain
Davis.[28] With minor variations, it was an oft-repeated pattern.

A Methodist, if he believed himself called to the ministry,
could apply to be taken on as a provisional minister—a licensed
preacher. Two to four years would then be spent in apprenticeship before ordination and assignment of an independent
circuit. Many remained as local preachers without seeking to
move on to full ordination in the itinerant ministry. For those
who sought full ordination the requirements, beyond the apprenticeship, were straight forward. In the words of the book of
Methodist church discipline, favorable responses to the following questions were necessary:

1. Do you know God as pardoning God? Have you the love of God abiding in you?
2. Have they gifts...Have they (in some tolerable degree) a clear, sound understanding...
3. Have they fruit? Are any truly convinced of sin and converted to God, by their preaching?[29]

Most of the ministers of the nineteenth century were educated in just this way. It was a system praised by contemporaries for making a minister, "a man of common sense and a man of the people."[30] It was also a system which fit with the demands of the Jacksonian era that the leader be one who was, "disciplined without having passed through the formal training..."[31] If the phenomenal growth of Methodism in the early nineteenth century is the yardstick, it was also a system which worked.

In 1816 a major reform took place in the Methodist apprenticeship system. The General Conference of that year called for a conference course of study which would guarantee that those learning on the circuit engage in a minimum amount of reading. According to the *Discipline* adopted at that conference:

It shall be the duty of the Bishops or of a committee which they may appoint, at each annual conference, to point out a course of reading and study proper to be pursued by candidates for the ministry: and the presiding elder, whenever such are presented to him, shall direct them to those studies which have been thus recommended—and before any candidate is received into full connexion, he shall give satisfactory evidence respecting his knowledge of those particular subjects which have been recommended to his consideration.[32]

Initially the course of reading was for the first two years of candidacy, but in time it was extended to a full four years.

Even before 1816 a similar pattern of education had prevailed in practice as Cartwright remembered:

We had at this early day [1804] no course of study prescribed, as at present; but William M'Kendree, afterward bishop but then my presiding elder, directed me to a proper course of reading and study. He selected books for me, both literary and theological; and every quarterly visit he made, he examined into my progress, and corrected my errors, if I had fallen into any. He delighted to instruct me in English grammar.[33]

The 1816 legislation made it the specific responsibility of the bishops to continue the work of such teachers as McKendree and ruled that "no candidate could be received into full connection until he had satisfactorily passed an examination on the course of study."[34]

The course of study was not adopted without opposition. Nathan Bangs, who played a crucial role in the adoption of the 1816 legislation, remembered that the "measures encountered great opposition from many delegates, and were debated through three or four days."[35] As late as 1844, a delegate at the General Conference argued against elaboration of the course of study, "Introduce this plan, and the preachers would become too scientific, and preach over the people's heads."[36] Any move which might make the preachers less dependent on the Spirit or less directly in touch with the common people—which might replace spontaneity with formalism—was bound to provoke opposition. And yet for the majority of Methodists the course of study combined with apprenticeship on the circuit seemed a safe balance.

When the Methodists split along sectional lines in 1844 the assignments of the readings were still left to the bishops and the regional annual conferences. By 1848 in the North and 1858 in the South, however, the course had been refined into a four-year series of readings with prescribed texts which were uniform through the connection.[37] The African Methodist Episcopal Church which had broken off from the parent body in 1804 listed the readings in its Discipline as early as 1844.[38]

The core of the study program was the Bible, the Methodist *Discipline* and *Hymnbook*, Wesley's *Sermons* and several books on doctrine, notably Watson's *Institutes*. Both the northern and southern connections also required a smattering of English grammar, logic, rhetoric, and history.[39] If the candidate was reasonably well-tutored in the "3r's" and read diligently through the program he could gain a respectable education. "The average circuit preacher was a man of few books," a twentieth-century Methodist historian claimed, "but he thoroughly absorbed those few. The books with which he was most familiar were the Bible, the *Discipline*, Wesley's *Sermons*, and Fletcher's *Appeal*."[40] As long as the system of circuits and circuit riders remained basic to Methodism's ministry, this combination of a course of study along with an apprenticeship on the circuit would be the mainstay of the denomination's theological education.

When the New Light party left the Presbyterian church in Kentucky in 1803 in a move which would eventually lead to the founding of the Disciples of Christ and when a second group of Kentucky and Tennessee Presbyterians formed their own separate Cumberland Presbyterian Church in 1810, issues regarding the proper theological education of ministers were among the crucial factors leading to the separation. In each case, those leaving left over several issues, but among them was, as Cumberland historians have rightly pointed out, "the question of education....a question of relaxing of the requirements for a *classical* education rather than of licensing and ordaining men who were illiterate."[41] The Cumberland Presbyterians had no intention of licensing illiterate preachers, although they were certainly accused of that by their opponents. On the other hand, they also had no intention of letting a situation continue in which many churches were without pastors, because too few potential ministers had mastered Latin and Greek as required by the Presbyterian church.[42]

In the case of the largest American denominations, the Methodists and Baptists, no split over issues of theological education took place. In Methodist circles this was because, in the early years, there was a strong consensus in favor of apprenticeship training and against specialized theological schooling. When schools of theology did emerge they were on the margins of the denomination so that those who supported them could do so while those who opposed them could ignore them. An even more flexible polity allowed Baptists to include a wide range of opinion regarding the best means of theological education. Baptists were free to work together in support of apprenticeship programs, colleges, or theological seminaries. They were equally free to ignore any of these since only the local

Baptist congregation could decide who was or was not qualified for ordained ministry.

These four groups—Baptists, Methodists, Disciples of Christ, and Cumberland Presbyterians had many significant differences among themselves. Baptists and Methodists regularly debated regarding their differing views of infant baptism and the importance of immersion. Cumberland Presbyterians continued to hold to most of the tenets of Presbyterianism, while the Disciples of Christ opposed all creeds but the Bible. But however much they might disagree on these issues—and the disagreements were often in the forefront of their interaction—they did agree on one thing. The insistence of the older Reformation churches—the Presbyterians, Congregationalists, and their allies—on a thorough classical education, including the Latin and Greek content of a college curriculum—simply made no sense in the conditions of the nation's fastest growing areas. They wanted ministers who were as well educated as possible. But the test of the education was the ability to lead the revival, to adapt to frontier conditions, and they did not mean to "cast off all the young preachers, because they had not learned Latin and Greek."[43]

In fact there was a clear tension running throughout all of the discussions of educational requirements for the ministry among these denominations. On the one hand, there was strong support for education—the insistence that as much education as possible was desirable for the young preachers, but that those with certain limitations, usually a lack of Latin and Greek, should still be ordained. On the other hand, there was a fear of certain kinds of education, education which was described as "artificial" or likely to "unfit" a candidate for ministry under frontier conditions. It was a tension which was never resolved, but continued to run through all of the discussions of ministerial education in the antebellum era.

This tension did not have to be thoroughly resolved, because another educational institution—the college—solved the issue. By attending college close to home, and by attending a college in which both clergy and laity were educated together, a future minister could receive the best of both worlds—as much of a classical education as possible, and an education linked to the same people who would make up future revival congregations. A structured educational experience could be made possible and yet be offered in a form which did not "unfit" one for ministry. It is no wonder that this institution had such popularity throughout the breadth of American Protestantism.

FOOTNOTES

[1] John A. Broadus, "Ministerial Education," in Sermons and Addresses (Baltimore: H. M. Wharton & Col, 1887), pp. 201-2.

[2] Charles G. Finney, Memoirs (New York: 1876), pp. 45-46.

[3] Ben M. Barrus, Milton L. Baughn, and Thomas H. Campbell, A People Called Cumberland Presbyterians (Memphis, TN: Frontier Press, 1972), pp. 50-51.

[4] Alexander Campbell, "The Clergy—No. IV," The Christian Baptist, Vol. 1 (January 5, 1824) republished ed. by D. S. Burnett (Cincinnati: American Christian Publication Society, 1854), p. 35.

[5] Riley Benjamin Montgomery, The Education of Ministers of the Disciples of Christ (St. Louis: The Bethany Press, 1931), p. 47.

[6] John William Ward, Andrew Jackson: Symbol for an Age (New York: Oxford University Press, 1953, p. 55.

[7] Andrew Jackson, 'Address to his Troops,' January 21, 1815, The Enquirer, February 22, 1815, cited in Ward, p. 46.

[8] A. Lacarriere Latour, Historical Memoir of the War in West Florida and Louisiana in 1814-1815, trans. H. P. Nugent (Philadelphia, 1816), cited in Ward, p. 47.

[9] Alexander Walker, Jackson and New Orleans: An Authentic Narrative of the Memorable Achievements of the American Army Under Andrew Jackson Before New Orleans in the Winter of 1814-'15 (New York, 1856), pp. 154-155, cited in Ward, p. 47.

[10] Journal of the General Conference of the Methodist Episcopal Church, South, 1854, p. 304.

[11] Journal of the General Conference, MECS, 1854, p. 307.

[12] The Doctrines and Discipline of the Methodist Episcopal Church 17th edition (New york: D. Hitt & T. Ware, 1814), p. 59. Hereafter cited as Discipline.

[13] G. W. Paschal, "Sandy Creek Church," in Encyclopedia of Southern Baptists, 2 vols. (Nashville: Broadman Press, 1958), Vol I, p. 185.

[14] Ibid.

[15] Alexander Campbell, "School of the Preachers," The Millennial Harbinger 6 (October, 1835): 478-479.

[16] Ibid.

[17] Alexander Campbell, "The School of the Preachers," *The Millenial Harbinger* 7 (January, 1836): 45-46.

[18] A. P. Jones to "Dear brother Campbell," *The Millennial Harbinger* n.s. 2 (December, 1838): 571-572.

[19] W. K. Pendleton, "Bethany College, Free Lectures for Ministers," *The Millennial Harbinger* 38 (January, 1867): 43-44.

[20] R. Milligan, "The Hiram Lectures," *The Millennial Harbinger* 37 (October, 1866): 451-452.

[21] "The Ministers' Institute, its Origin, Method, and Practical Utility, together with an abstract of the minutes of the Fourth Session of the Illinois Ministers' Institute, held at Chicago, July 10-20, 1866" (Chicago: Church and Goodman Publishers, 1866), p. 8.

[22] Ibid.

[23] *Discipline*, 1814, p. 34.

[24] Peter Cartwright, *Autobiography* (New York: Carlton and Porter, 1857), p. 79.

[25] William Henry Milburn, *Ten Years of Preacher Life* (New York: Derby & Jackson, 1859), pp. 64-65.

[26] R. M. Wyant, "Without the Seminary," in *Semi-Centennial Celebration: Garrett Biblical Institute* (Evanston: n.p., 1906), p. 195.

[27] "Letter of B. H. Pierson to Mrs. Silas Newton Davies," quoted in Barrus, Baugh, and Campbell, p. 195.

[28] Ibid.

[29] *Discipline* (1814), pp. 44-45.

[30] Thos. M. Finney, *The Life and Labors of Enoch Mather Marvin, Late Bishop of the Methodist Episcopal Church, South* (St. Louis: James H. Chambers, 1880), p. 169.

[31] Ward, p. 47.

[32] *Discipline* (1816), p. 34.

[33] Cartwright, p. 78.

[34] Paul Neff Garber, *The Romance of American Methodism* (Greensboro, NC: The Piedmont Press, 1931), pp. 242-243.

[35] Abel Stevens, *Life and Times of Nathan Bangs, D.D.* (New York: Published by Carlton & Porter, 1863), p. 214.

[36] *Journal of the General Conference of the Methodist Episcopal Church, 1844* (New York: Carlton & Phillips, 1856), p. 216.

[37] While northern Methodists began listing all readings in the *Discipline* in 1848, the southern Methodists only began that process in 1878. However, after the reforms of 1858, the readings were standardized and published throughout the southern connection. See for example the "Course of Study," *Nashville Christian Advocate* 23, October 1869, p. 3.

[38] *The Doctrine and Discipline of the African Methodist Episcopal Church* (Brooklyn, NY: Piercy & Reed, 1844), p. 251.

[39] Charles T. Thrift, Jr., "The History of Theological Education in the Methodist Episcopal Church, South, 1845-1915," (B.D./A.M. thesis, Duke University,

1933), pp. 39-40; also Garber, p. 243; *Discipline*, North (1848); *Discipline*, South (1858). Don Gustafson and Myron Yonker, "A Survey of the Course of Study in American Methodism," prepared for Dr. David C. Shipley, fall, 1958 (typewritten paper in the files of Methodist Board of Education, Nashville, Tennessee). Gustafson and Yonker have traced all those books published at any time in the Course of Study and charted the time they spent on either the northern or southern reading lists.

[40] William Warren Sweet, *Methodism in American History* (Cincinnati: Methodist Book Concern, 1933), p. 147.

[41] Barrus, Baughn, and Campbell, *A People Called Cumberland Presbyterians*, p. 154.

[42] Ibid, pp. 50 ff.

[43] Ibid, p. 59.

Chapter V

NOTHING CAN SAVE US BUT AN ABLE MINISTRY
AND NONE CAN BE HAD
BUT THROUGH [COLLEGE] EDUCATION

John Early, a Methodist preacher and later to be the first chair of the Board of Trustees at Randolph-Macon College was a worried man in 1822. At that time, he was serving as the chair of the committee to examine candidates for the ministry for the Methodist's Virginia Conference. And the candidates were not doing well. Early's handwritten notes in the Randolph-Macon archives report the results of the examinations:

> John F. Andrew, on Divinity, good; on History, tolerable; English Grammar, deficient; on Geography, deficient. Robert Wilkinson, on Divinity, good; on History, deficient; English, Grammar, ____; on Geography, lacking.[1]

The list continued, but in that year and in subsequent years, the number of deficients was far too large. The apprenticeship pattern, including the conference course of study which Early's Methodist church had formally established in 1816,[2] was not working. Something new had to be found.

Nationally Methodists had already begun working on a solution to this problem. At the 1820 General Conference of the denomination it was recommended to all of the regional annual conferences, "to establish, as soon as practicable, literary institutions, under their own control...."[3] The conference also revised the *Discipline* to allow teaching in such a school as valid itinerant work, allowing ministers as well as lay people to serve on the faculty.[4] Four years later, the next General Conference added more urgency to the request. After that the idea of Methodist academies and colleges caught on quickly, north and south. In Virginia, Hezekiah Leigh, a minister, and Gabriel P. Disosway, a layman, began pushing for a school. Providing a college education for Methodists, future ministers and future laypeople, would solve the problem of the high number of "deficients" on the examinations. The standards for the ministry could be raised, while at the same time avoiding an issue highly controversial among Methodists—specialized training for ministers alone.[5]

The almost universal opposition among early nineteenth-century Methodists, frontier Baptists, Cumberland Presbyterians, and Disciples of Christ to theological seminaries did not extend to academies (often called seminaries) or colleges. Although Peter Cartwright, for one, spoke vigorously against professional education for ministers, he also played a major role in the founding of several academies and colleges in the Midwest.

Academies and colleges were not new as a means of theological education. They had long served that purpose in the east, and they were built for that purpose in the west, not only by the revivalists, but by their bitterest opponents. But for the new evangelicals, for the nation's fastest growing denominations, colleges could be adapted especially well to fit their unique demands. These schools could deal with the often-voiced concern for raising the educational level of the second generation preachers without departing from the understanding of the nature of the ministry which had emerged among these groups. In college, future preachers could be educated along with tomorrow's politicians, editors, farmers and others. They would not be separated from their own region or daily contact with lay people. In a sense these newer denominations were attempting through their colleges to do what Harvard and William & Mary had done in the seventeenth century—educate all leaders in a common curriculum. But they did it in a way that was true to the spirit of nineteenth-century evangelicalism.[6]

The differences between colleges and theological seminaries are important for understanding of the nature of the ministry among these denominations. A college education, unlike that of a seminary, included no specialized training for the ministry. Future clergy and laity were educated together. This allowed those preparing for the ministry to remain amateurs, amateurs with a higher standard of education than their predecessors, but still amateurs in their links with the laity and their dependence on divine inspiration, rather than professional status, as the key to their power.

When Alexander Campbell opened Bethany College on his Virginia farm in 1840 to serve the Disciples of Christ, he shared the same vision of collegiate education as his Methodist colleagues. In an extravagant claim for the new college, he wrote:

> Bethany College is the only College known to us in the civilized world, founded upon the Bible. It is not a theological school, founded upon human theology, nor a school of divinity, founded upon the Bible; but a literary and scientific institution, founded upon the Bible as the basis of all true science and true learning....Those destined for the ministry of the Word, are thus furnished with all the grand materials of their future profession: and those assigned to other professions in life, are prepared to enjoy themselves in the richest of all possessions—a mind enlightened with Divine Revelation, and the history of men impartially drawn by the hands of the greatest masters that ever spoke or wrote.[7]

The old institution of the college was being remodeled to fit a new situation; a new understanding of Christian ministry. A case study of the founding of two of these colleges—the first two founded by Methodists—will shed light on the reasons the newer denominations put so many of their resources into college building.

There is, to this day, a friendly rivalry between Randolph-Macon and Wesleyan as to which was founded first. The Virginia school received its state charter in 1830, but did not open for classes until 1832. Its Connecticut counterpart received its charter in May of 1831 and started classes in September of that same year.[8] The rivalry makes the point all the better—both schools were founded at essentially the same time, and for essentially the same reasons. Methodists were worried about the state of the ministry. They had developed a unique understanding of the nature of the Christian ministry, the itinerant circuit rider whose ultimate preparation was his own understanding of the call of the Holy Spirit, and whose ultimate test was the ability to convert sinners—and win them to the Methodist fold. But by 1830, they were dissatisfied with this system. Specifically they were troubled by three things—the educational standards of those entering the itineracy, competition from other denominations for some of the best of the Methodist ministers, and maintaining a clear identity for those who were engaged in the work. As an examination of the founding of these two schools will show, the college provided an effective means of addressing each of these issues, while at the same time maintaining the understanding of the ministry which was at the core of Methodism.

Standards
In late 1824, Hezekiah Leigh and Gabriel P. Disosway helped to frame the first appeal for their school, an "Address, To the Members and Friends of the Methodist Episcopal Church." Among the reasons given for founding the school was their hope "to afford young men, who give evidence of their being called by the Lord Jesus Christ to preach the Gospel, and that they possess the gifts and graces of the Holy Spirit, an opportunity to obtain important qualifications for the Ministry."[9]

Leigh and Disosway also immediately contacted John Early,[10] and the three persuaded the Virginia Conference of Methodists to make application for a charter and then per-

suaded the Virginia Legislature to grant it. After some controversy, the General Assembly of Virginia, on February 3, 1830,
granted a charter for the school which included Hezekiah Leigh
and John Early—Disosway had moved north by this time—
among the trustees.[11] After a search for funds and a faculty,
the school opened two years later in 1832. A solution to Early's
complaint about the deficient preparation of candidates for the
ministry was at hand. As the school's first president summarized the conviction of those who worked to establish it, "nothing can save us but an able ministry, and this can not be had
but through education."[12] While some would remind Olin that
less educated ministers could also save souls, by 1830 most
Methodists were ready to accept the fact that the work might be
carried on more effectively when those ministers were better
educated.

The experience in Connecticut was very similar. The 1820
and 1824 resolutions urging literary academies had been read
there, and the same worries about the state of future ministers
were present. In 1828, at the next quadrennial General Conference, Willbur Fisk, the principal of Massachusetts' Wilbraham
Academy chaired the Committee on Education. He used this
occasion to push for the establishment of Methodist colleges.
Colleges were, Fisk insisted, the ideal educational institution for
Methodism because they would raise the standards for the
ministry without compromising the nature of the ministry as
understood by Methodists.

Fisk reminded his fellow Methodists that colleges were
useful in raising the standards of the ministry in their denomination. At the same time, Fisk insisted, "We do not indeed
profess to educate young men and train them up specifically for
the ministry." Fisk wanted to make it clear that in founding
colleges, Methodists would not be engaging in what they continued to accuse Congregationalists and Presbyterians of doing,
"manufacturing preachers." But, Fisk went on:

> ...it will be readily seen, that, as our ministers are raised up
> mostly from among ourselves, their literary character will
> vary according to the general character of the church.[13]

103

Throughout his career, Fisk would continue to be a major proponent of the improving the "literary character" of Methodist ministers and Methodist laypeople by founding colleges which both could attend together. In this way the education of many leaders would be improved while the specific needs for higher standards in ministerial education would also be addressed. He continually worried that, "our ministry is in many respects greatly deficient; and what is to me a matter of deeper and more fearful interest, that deficiency will be felt more in twenty years than it now is, from the fact that, while society in general is advancing, we receive ministers on our old standards, and educate them in the old way...."[14] Of course, Fisk would not settle for the old ways—the college provided a new solution to the problem and he intended to use it.

Fisk found an important ally in his desire for a college in another Methodist minister, Laban Clark. While Fisk worked to persuade his colleagues in New England, Clark did the same in the New York conference, and both Methodist conferences agreed to the joint support of a school in 1829.[15] As they began looking for a campus, the decision to close an existing military school in Middletown, Connecticut, led Clark to conclude, "there is a fair opening, in my judgment, for a school of higher order in Middletown to embrace youth of both sexes.[16] It was a fair opening indeed. Within a year, funds had been raised, the campus secured, a charter granted, and classes were in operation at Wesleyan University with Fisk as the first president and Clark as the chairman of the Board of Trustees.[17] Fisk would have the opportunity to devote the rest of his life to raising the standards of the Methodist ministry, to answer the need, as he described it, of those who insist, "Do not send us uneducated boys but men—men who can instruct us." Fisk planned to ensure that the next generation of ministers would be "better educated before they are imposed on the people."[18]

College founders like Early and Leigh in Virginia or Fisk and Clark in the northeast were a group of people who shared a concern about the quality of the ministry in their denomination. The fact that they were able to gain the support to move so quickly is an important indication that in their concern for ministerial standards, they had struck a responsive chord.

A concern for standards, for measuring their potential ministers against their own ideal for ministry, was not, however, the only motivating factor for those who struggled to found colleges. There was also another standard, more clearly defined, against which to measure themselves—other Protestant denominations. And in this race, also, they did not intend for the Methodists to lag behind.

Stephen Olin, the first president of Randolph-Macon before he moved on to serve as Fisk's successor as president of Wesleyan, spoke for the founders of both schools when he said of his students:

> They mean to do good—to teach or preach, or neither as God wills. They are just such men as the Church wants and must have—men who will be educated somewhere, and will exert influence in the world—for us and for Christ, if we will train them—against both, probably, if we will not. They are children of Methodist families—ours by birth-right, by baptism, and therefore a hundred-fold more likely to become pious under our training than under that of any other....My conclusion is, that the Methodist Episcopal Church can not dispense with such an instrument. She must educate her own youth, and those of her adherents, or prove false to her trust, and lose them—and generally they will be lost to others.[19]

What Olin said, might have been said by virtually any of the founders of the first Methodist colleges. While there was some expression of the fear of the secularism of some schools—especially the University of Virginia—the primary fear among all the founders seems to have been that if they did not provide an opportunity for a college education under Methodist auspices, their children would find it under the tutelage of other denominations, and stay with them.[20]

In a review of Hezekiah Leigh's life, W.H. Moore was quite clear that one of the main factors in Leigh's devotion to Randolph-Macon was that he, "saw the disastrous effects of educating our young people in colleges of other denominations, or, worse than that, of educating them in colleges where religion is ignored."[21] Fisk's wife likewise remembered that her husband,

105

"felt deeply in his own experience what they [Methodist youth] must suffer in institutions not under religious influence."[22] And Fisk, himself, defended Wesleyan by arguing that, "Our children before were exposed to be sent to schools, where they heard the religion of their fathers despised and spoken against."[23] The consensus was clear. Methodists needed colleges under their own control. Without them, they would lose the educated leadership, and especially the educated clerical leadership on which they were dependent in their struggle to survive and prosper among the competing claims of early nineteenth century Protestant rivalry.

Competition for these college founders, however, was not merely with other denominations. There was also competition among Methodists to have a college for their own conference. Once a school was organized, its supporters argued vigorously as the trustees of Wesleyan did, "To divide our strength on several Colleges for the sake of gratifying local interest and sectional feeling, will produce certain failure, and defeat the noble design of taking an elevated stand in the republic of letters."[24] But then the representatives of the New York and New England conferences who wrote that letter already had their school. They were trying to persuade representatives of neighboring conferences to support them rather than competing. They would not succeed. As Daniel Boorstin has argued so persuasively when he coined the phrase, "booster college," nineteenth century American higher education was a diffused and competitive phenomenon, with many centers of action.[25]

Thus, in 1834, while he was president of Randolph-Macon, Stephen Olin found himself in Georgia asking the support of Georgia Methodists for their neighboring conference's school. But as one of those who attended the conference remembered the debates, "a new idea had been thrown into our midst."[26] Georgia meant to have a college for itself. Olin protested sharply, writing in 1835, "I regret to hear of the Georgia Conference College. It is said they propose to take the endowment pledged to this college. This I think impossible as it would be a breach of faith to us and to the donors."[27] But plead as he might, the direction was set, "that Georgia needed a college of her own—ought to have it, must have it, would have it...."[28]

106

Emory University opened in Atlanta in 1836. Even among Methodists, competition won out over cooperation. Every conference, it seemed, wanted its own college.

In addition to town boosterism and denomination booster-ism, college founding was fueled by conference boosterism. Indeed each form of competition supported the other. Georgia Methodists, after all, were not only about to compete with a Methodist school in Virginia, but also with Georgia Baptists who were opening their own school, Mercer University, in Macon, Georgia within a year.[29] Such competitive emotions may not have led to careful planning, but they certainly served well to provide a badly needed source of energy for the planting of the schools.

Identity

The last reason for the founding of these colleges is the hardest to define precisely, for the founders did not discuss it as openly or as clearly. But if one reads between the lines in their writings, the theme emerges quite clearly. Antebellum Method-ists, like others of their generation, were increasingly concerned with questions of their personal and professional identity.[30]

Young Methodists, like others, wanted the professional identity which a college education provided and if the Methodist church would not provide it, others would. This was the regu-larly repeated warning of Olin and others that, "The ranks of our ministry were often impoverished by young men of piety and promise going out among others to seek literary advantages which we could not give them, and finally connecting them-selves with other ecclesiastical bodies."[31] Methodism needed to keep these ambitious youth.

This issue lent special urgency to the competition with other denominations. Methodist college advocates argued that in the schools of other denominations, "the whole influence was thrown against Methodist theology and usages....At last, in self-defense, Methodism was obliged to build her own seminaries and colleges."[32] Earlier generations of Methodists might have simply argued for staying away from college. But in the 1820s and 30s, the college founders had a clear sense that the best of those who might be attracted to the ministry in the future would be those who would insist on a college degree for themselves. They needed to be able to find such training in the Methodist fold. Again, Olin spoke for many in insisting, "I say the Church must train its own youth if it would save them—if it would retain them—if it would have polished shafts in its quiver—bold champions to meet the enemy in the gate."[33] One of Randolph-Macon's historians is also correct in noting that ministerial candidates were bent on "pursuing higher education because they wanted it for its own sake."[34] There were considerations beyond the best preparation for future ministry. After all, as James MacLachlan has persuasively argued for antebellum America, "in a rapidly shifting society such as the United States, marks of permanent status have always been hard to come by: An 'A.B.' after one's name was certainly permanent."[35]

The founding of a Methodist college offered a new professional identity not only for future graduates. It also created a new career for Methodist ministers—that of college professor and president. If one examines the careers of the first presidents of each of these schools, this new career identity—this new understanding of a kind of ministry—becomes evident. In 1820, the Methodist General Conference, as a means of encouraging the establishment of academies and colleges, specifically provided that teaching might be an appropriate role for a Methodist preacher, something previously prohibited.[36] It was an important opportunity for a few. Willbur Fisk was an ordained preacher, but not in active service when he became principal of Wilbraham Academy, the post from which he moved to Wesleyan.[37] The story is told that his mother, a pious Methodist herself, did not approve, "She was afraid he would lose his spirituality—She said that she did not think it right for him to leave the Word of God to serve tables."[38] But Fisk was, in fact, moving from a partial retirement, back into more active service, and a service where he argued he had "the hope of benefiting the ministry the more."[39]

Similarly, Olin wrote of his first college teaching appointment at Congregationalist Middlebury College, "It will give me opportunity to preach as often, probably, as my health will admit under any circumstances; it will secure me a comfortable support, a useful and respectable station in society, and it will restore me to friends whom I love, and habits which I reverence."[40] This was an honest statement. It is very hard to imagine either Fisk or Olin as successful Methodist circuit riders. Neither was ever in robust health. They were also both, as Olin admitted, concerned with a respectable station and comfortable habits. They were academics by taste and they liked the social status. The founding of Methodist colleges gave them an opportunity to reconcile their own identity with their commitments as Methodist ministers. They, and many of their successors, would jump at the chance.

While only a few college founders could become members of the faculty there was a role for others also—they became the trustees of the new institutions, and this too gave them a new identity in their own eyes and that of their peers. While ministers like John Early, Hezekiah Leigh and Laban Clark continued throughout their careers as itinerant preachers, they were also itinerants who were recognized as the leaders among their companions, and their position on a college trustee board added to their status. Much later, James Brice noted of Americans that, "In a country where

there is no titled class, no landed class, no military class, the chief distinction which popular sentiment can lay hold of as raising one set of persons above another is the character of their occupation, the degree of culture it implies, the extent to which it gives them an honourable prominence."[41]

The "honourable prominence" of serving on a college board of trustees was especially useful when it lead the same board to confer the often coveted D.D. degree. At the 1832 General Conference, Methodists found themselves debating "the subject of our preachers accepting the honorary title of D.D."[42] But the discussion was tabled. In a country where there was no official rank, and in a denomination whose polity moved in the same direction, new forms of status seemed necessary. To be a trustee or a D.D. was as close as many of these founders might ever come to a Protestant equivalent of a Monsignoriate. It was an opportunity not be be regarded lightly.

Other Examples

When the General Conference of the Methodist Episcopal Church created a new Conference for the state of Indiana in 1832, one of the new conference's first moves was to begin a process which would lead to the founding of what would be Indiana Asbury or DePauw University. For the conference leaders it was clear that a college could serve their understanding of the nature of the Methodist ministry—a school which prepared future itinerants under Methodist auspices and in mixed company with their future hearers. As they began to create the school, the conference members were careful to announce that:

> We are aware that when a Conference Seminary is named, some of our preachers and many of our people suppose we are about to establish a manufactory in which preachers are to be made. But nothing is farther from our views....[43]

The Methodist distrust of "manufacturing preachers" continued to be strong enough that it was essential for these Indiana college founders to assure their constituency that the proposed school was for all, not for the exclusive education of ministers. They also made it clear that they recognized that only the Holy Spirit could make ministers—that is that they still shared a common understanding of the nature of the Methodist ministry. Having done this the conference leaders felt free to go ahead with their plans. Within five years, by 1837, they had a functioning school. The college was being remolded to fit the needs of the Methodist understanding of the nature of the ministry. As with the earlier schools, Indiana's Methodist college would serve as a school which would prepare another generation of Methodist preachers, trained to high standards, but in the company of the laity, loyal to Methodism and the itineracy, and clear in their identity as both Methodists and educated citizens.

For all of their support of college foundations, however, it cannot be said that there was a widely accepted Methodist policy towards college education. Methodists fought among themselves with great energy over every issue related to the education of their ministers and laity. The stakes were high. The heart of the Methodist understanding of the ministry, the itinerancy, was at risk. While high standards were seen as essential by many Methodists, many others also worried that any attempt to train ministers obstructed the direct inspiration of the Holy Spirit. This vacillation did not take place only between different factions of Methodism, but in the minds of individual Methodists. Thus Peter Cartwright, who helped to found a number of Methodist colleges, also spoke for many of his contemporaries when he said:

> When God wants great and learned men in the ministry, how easy it is for him to overtake a learned sinner, and, as Saul of Tarsus, shake him a while over hell, then knock the scales from his eyes, and without any previous theological training, send him out straightway to preach Jesus and the resurrection.[44]

Educating future preachers always seemed to some to be dangerously close to trifling with God's call. Of course, the logic of Cartwright's position would be that the only well educated Methodists would be those who came to their faith later in life; after gaining an education while still unconverted sinners. Methodists did not adhere to such a position. For those youth who were sure of their faith, but not of their vocation, college was clearly encouraged. Also for those who believed themselves called to the ministry at a young age, college was desirable. But once a person was clear of the call to the ministry, especially if that person were past normal college age, the needs of the times seemed so great that most agreed that the work should begin immediately. Spending time in study at that point always smacked of a vain desire to appear more cultivated than the ministry required.[45]

The career of Thomas Goodwin, the first college graduate to join the Indiana conference, illustrates this ambivalence. Although the conference had begun plans to found a college at its birth in 1832, and had supported Indiana Asbury after it opened in 1837, when the first graduate of that school entered the conference membership in 1838, the sentiments against college-educated preachers came to the fore. Rather than be accused of favoring a college graduate over other ministers, the presiding elders consistently gave Goodwin marginal assignments. Eventually he left the itinerancy in frustration to serve the church as an editor rather than face the hostility of his colleagues to his college degree.[46]

In time, however, experiences like Goodwin's became more and more rare as more and more graduates of Methodist colleges entered the active ministry. In the years immediately after the founding of Randolph-Macon and Wesleyan, Methodists either founded or adopted Allegheny College and Dickinson College in Pennsylvania, McKendree College in Illinois, Emory University and Wesleyan College in Georgia, and as well as Indiana Asbury.[47]

By this point in their history, most Methodists realized that they had few options left if they wanted to remain a major denomination among Protestants. Writing in denominational journals in the 1830s, John Durbin argued:

> These young men, generally the most promising of our best families, will be educated somewhere. If there be not proper and elevated institutions under our own patronage, they will be sent to others. What is the consequence?....As might be expected, many became alienated, or were drawn from us. The ranks of our ministry were often impoverished by young men of piety and promise going out among others to seek literary advantages which we could not give them, and finally connecting themselves with other ecclesiastical bodies....[48]

Many who might be important and influential lay leaders in Methodism, many who might be great preachers, were going to the colleges of other denominations. At the same time, colleges did not pose a real threat to the Methodist understanding of ministry. While there was the fear of trifling with God's call, education in a Methodist college did not threaten to cut a preacher off from other Methodists—clergy and laity. And a college education, because it could be used either in the ministry or elsewhere, did not smack of "manufacturing preachers" as did education in an institution devoted only to that purpose. As a college education became more and more the mark of a leader, and as ownership of a college became more and more the symbol of a denomination's arrival, Methodists found themselves increasingly comfortable with the institution.

Perhaps nowhere was the symbolic power of owning a college more clearly illustrated than in the African Methodist Episcopal Church. The Ohio Conference of the A.M.E. founded a school, Union Seminary, in 1845, when most Blacks were still in slavery.[49] While that school never flourished, the next attempt was far more successful. In 1856, the white Methodist Episcopal Church in the north founded Wilberforce University near Xenia, Ohio, to serve Blacks. Seven years later the university was sold to the A.M.E. for $10,000. Purchasing a school during the Civil War for that amount of money, and then raising tens of thousands of additional dollars to support the school in the immediate post-war years, in a denomination which was largely made up of desperately poor people, indicates something of the importance vested in the ownership of a college. The school's first Black president, Daniel Payne, could boast proudly, "Hundreds of its under-graduates have become successful teachers and preachers, and others are to be found in various fields of usefulness."[50]

A similar pattern was duplicated in other denominations. While Brown University was founded in Rhode Island as a result of the pre-revolutionary awakening, it was only after the Revolution that Baptists began a major drive towards college founding. Perhaps the most important Baptist leader in college founding was Richard Furman of South Carolina who began in the mid-1790s to urge the Charleston Association to send ministerial candidates to Rhode Island College for further training.[51] After 1800 Furman also worked with two New England Baptists, Luther Rice and Adoniram Judson to found the national Baptist Triennial Convention to support both education and mission work.[52] Rice went on to help found a Baptist college at Washington, D.C. in 1821, which eventually became George Washington University.[53] Furman also helped to found a school in his native South Carolina. While Furman Academy did not survive the Civil War, it provided the model for a number of other Baptist college which spread throughout the south.[54]

Many of these new colleges were established in what was then the western frontier. They fit the needs of the ministry there too well not to be developed. Thus the six major colleges founded in Illinois between 1827 and the Civil War were, ac-

113

cording to Timothy Smith, "more indigenous to the West than is often supposed."[55] Shurtleff, McKendree, Illinois, Illinois Wesleyan, Illinois State University, and Knox College were all established by Protestants intent on providing a higher quality education, both for future ministers and for the population in general, especially those who would practice the other professions of medicine, law and teaching. In each case, "the zeal of ordinary Westerners"[56] stirred by the awakening led them to develop institutions of education which would train leaders for the future.

The Disciples of Christ and the Cumberland Presbyterians followed similar patterns. The Disciples leader Alexander Campbell, who had begun an academy known as "Buffalo Seminary" as early as 1818,[57] opened Bethany College in Bethany, Virginia in 1840, as he insisted to ensure, "in raising up me for the field when I shall be absent from this planet.... preachers worthy of the gospel and of the age, and teachers worthy of the Bible and the Church."[58] Cumberland College opened in 1826, and Cumberland University in 1852.[59]

In all of these cases denominational self-interest and altruism, combined with land speculation and regional pride to create a series of institutions across the nation which would continue to be the major agencies for higher education for generations. When a Methodist committee on education declared in 1840 that the "advantages of education are most wisely diffused and certainly secured, by multiplying institutions of learning,"[60] they may have gone against the conventional wisdom of later educators who hoped for quality in a small number of schools, but they clearly represented the belief of their own generation in the possibilities of college education— theological and otherwise— spreading to the greatest number.[61]

The curriculum of these colleges had little to do with specific education for the ministry. Prior to the Civil War, with a few notable exceptions, the college curriculum did not change significantly in America. The curriculum of a classical liberal education had been set in the universities of Europe. The American pattern was copied from that, first at Harvard and William & Mary, and later across the nation. A liberal, classical education was seen as the best training for leadership, whether that leadership was to be in church, politics, or another profession.

Evidence for the classical nature of western colleges can be found in the early admission requirements at Indiana Asbury:

> A knowledge of Geography, English Grammar, Arithmetic, First lessons in Algebra, Latin Grammar, Historia Sacra, Caesar's Commentaries, Virgil, Greek Grammar, and Greek Testament.[62]

If a student had to be able to read the Greek testament and the Latin Virgil in the original tongues to gain admission to college, what did one study after that? In 1842, Francis Wayland, sometime President of Brown University, described the antebellum curriculum:

> In Latin select portions of Livy, Tacitus, Horace, Cicero de Oratore, Juvenal; — In Greek, select portions of Xenophon's Anabasis, Memorabilia, the Illiad, some of the tragedies of Sophocles and Eschylus, with Demosthenes' Oration for the Crown...

In addition there was Mathematics, Natural Philosophy, Natural Science, Rhetoric, Logic, Moral Philosophy, Political Economy, Analogy, and the American Constitution.[63] Once the commitment was made by some Methodists to found and use colleges, questions of curriculum, it seemed, were secondary. Most Americans knew what a college curriculum included. Some schools might do a better job of following it than others; some individuals might argue that it was totally irrelevant, while others insisted on its importance; but few argued about the content of the curriculum itself. Serious efforts on a meaningful scale to alter the system did not come until after the Civil War.

While the image of pious Methodist or Baptist farm boys laboring over Livy and Tacitus is appealing, that is not all that happened in the colleges. As in all circumstances the formal curriculum was far from the limits of the education to be gained. Students also got to know other students from other parts of their region, formed their own student associations, and talked with the faculty. Nearly all of the faculty were also preachers who could not only lecture on the classics, but also tell stories of their own experiences as Methodist itinerants or Baptist, Cumberland or Disciples preachers. Thus while the college curriculum did not directly address issues of ministry, and did not offer the practical experiences of an apprenticeship, the college student did have many opportunities in the course of four years in a small institution to be exposed to the mores and folk tales of a particular tradition.

Some of the colleges were relatively successful in their goal of educating both preachers and lay people. When Indiana Asbury's first president, Mathew Simpson, was elected a Bishop and left the college in 1848, he could count a total of sixty-one graduates during the school's first decade. Among those graduates, 18 were ministers, 18 lawyers, 7 medical doctors, and the rest in business, banking, editing, and farming plus one California gold prospector.[64] A far more significant statistic, however, was the size of the student body in that year—268.[65] While the school had been growing, the disparity between the 1848 enrollment and the list of alumni also indicates that the vast majority of students did not finish, but studied at the school for a year or two and then moved on. Statistics are not available as to how many of those who left without a degree entered the ministry, but there is no reason to assume that the proportions were not similar to graduates. The result is that far more Methodist preachers experienced some exposure to the classical curriculum, along with whatever other training they might receive, than any list of college graduates would show.

Academies and colleges—and the classical curriculum— were not new as a means of theological education. Certainly they were not invented by the Methodists, Baptists, Cumberland Presbyterians or Disciples. Neither was the ideal of educating future ministers and lay leaders in the same classroom. Harvard and William and Mary had begun that process in America two centuries earlier. Still something new had happened in the course of the first half of the nineteenth century. A distinctive pattern of theological education had been formed. The Methodists, the Disciples of Christ, the Cumberland Presbyterians, and the vast majority of Baptists had broken away from the tradition among all American Protestants up to that time of insisting upon the ideal of a thorough classical education prior to ordination. While ministers might be educated along with laypeople at colonial Harvard, there was only one route to the ministry—through the college. Now the college was only one option among many. Apprenticeship with a circuit rider, private study through a course of study, and if possible, attending a liberal arts college might all be desirable, might all help to raise the standards for the ministry, but they were only some of the ingredients in the pattern of preparation for ministry. Unlike the colonial pattern, in which the core of the understanding of the ministry included the classically educated community leader and teacher, the new model of minister was the preacher who was a "man of the people," and whose primary role was to save souls through preaching. A classical education might contribute to that role, or it might not, but it was no longer essential.

FOOTNOTES

¹John Early, chairman, "Report of the Examining Committee, Course of Study, 1822," handwritten ms., John Early papers, Walter Hines Page Library, Randolph-Macon College, Ashland, Virginia. See also James E. Scanlon, *Randolph-Macon College: A Southern History, 1825-1967* (Charlottesville, VA: The University Press of Virginia, 1983), p. 20. I am deeply indebted to Professor Scanlon for sharing this material with me prior to publication.

²*Journal of the General Conference, 1816*, p. 151, in *Journals of the General Conference of the Methodist Episcopal Church*, Volume I, 1796-1836 (New York: Carlton & Phillips, 1855).

³*Journal of the General Conference, 1820*, p. 208; *Journal of the General Conference, 1824*, p. 295.

⁴William Warren Sweet, *Methodism in American History* (Cincinnati: Methodist Book Concern, 1933), p. 211.

⁵Scanlon's study provides a good discussion of the ambivalence of Methodists regarding specialized training for the ministry, and especially their opposition to separate institutions for that training. See also Stephen Olin to the Rev. Mr. Landon, Leicester, Sept. 4, 1834, in Stephen Olin, *The Life and Letters*, 2 vols. (New York: Harper & Brothers, 1853), Vol. 1, p. 182.

⁶See chapter one of this study for the development of colleges in colonial America.

⁷Alexander Campbell, "Bethany College," *The Millennial Harbinger* ser.3, 7 (May, 1850): 291-93.

⁸Scanlon, p. 48.

⁹"Address, To the Members and Friends of the Methodist Episcopal Church," January 13, 1825, printed copy, Walter Hines Page Library, Randolph-Macon College.

¹⁰Gabriel P. Disosway to "Dear Bro. Early," Petersburg, Jan. 17, 1835, handwritten ms., Walter Hines Page Library, Randolph- Macon College.

¹¹Richard Irby, *History of Randolph-Macon College, Virginia* (Richmond: Whittet & Shepperson, 1898), pp. 10-15; se also James M. Becker, "Was Randolph-Macon Different? Revivalism, Sectionalism, and the Academic Tradition: The Methodist Mission in Higher Education, 1830-1880," unpublished Ph.D. dissertation, the University of North Carolina at Chapel Hill, for a useful discussion of the political struggles involved in obtaining a charter for this Methodist school from the Virginia legislature.

[12] Stephen Olin to the Rev. Mr. Landon, Leicester, Sept. 4, 1834, in Stephen Olin, *The Life and Letters,* 2 vols (New York: Harper & Brothers, 1853, Vol 1, p. 182.

[13] Willbur Fisk, Chairman, "Report of the Committee on Education," included with reports on the May, 1828 General Conference of the Methodist Episcopal Church printed in *Christian Advocate and Journal*, New York, June 13, 1828, pp. 2-3. Fisk returned again and again to this issue of training future preachers along with other students. He argued that to try a separate institution for preachers would "raise the popular cry in our Church against all our literary institutions," and he argued that, "It is the general opinion with us that this instruction can be better given in the literary institutions than in any separate school: this is *decidedly* my opinion." In Joseph Holdich, *The Life of Willbur Fisk* (New York: Harper & Brothers, 1842), pp. 306-307.

[14] Willbur Fisk to My Dear Brother [Rev. Martin P. Parks], Middletown, December 17, 1833, in Holdich, p. 305.

[15] Carl F. Price, *Wesleyan's First Century* (Middletown: Wesleyan University, 1932), pp. 22-25.

[16] Laban Clark to Dear Bro Judson, Oct. 11, 1830, handwritten letter, Laban Clark Papers, Olin Library, Wesleyan University, Middletown, Connecticut. Wesleyan was, in fact, an all male school until 1872 and Randolph-Macon was an all male school through the establishment of its now better known adjunct, Randolph-Macon Woman's College in 1891. See Roberta D. Cornelius, *The History of Randolph-Macon Woman's College* (Chapel Hill: The University of North Carolina Press, 1951).

[17] Price, pp. 22-32.

[18] Willbur Fisk, "Report of New England Missionary Society to New England Conference, 1833," cited in David H. Markle, "Willbur Fisk, Pioneer Methodist Educator," unpublished Ph.D. dissertation, Yale University, 1935.

[19] Olin, Life and Letters, Vol. II, pp. 84-85.

[20] Becker, pp. 45-46.

[21] W. H. Moore, "An Historical Oration on the Life and Labors of Rev. Hezekiah G. Leigh," December 8, 1896, printed pamphlet in the Walter Hines Page Library, Randolph-Macon College.

[22] Ruth Fisk, "Notes of Mrs. Ruth Fisk regarding her husband," handwritten ms., Fisk papers, Olin Library, Wesleyan University, p. 16.

[23] Willbur Fisk in the Christian Advocate and Journal, New York, Feb. 13, 1835, cited in Markle, p. 252.

[24] L. Clark, J. Lindsey, C.K. True, "The Board of Trustees and Visitors of the Wesleyan University, to the Members and Friends of the Methodist E. Church, within the bounds of the Northern and Eastern Annual Conferences," Middletown, Conn., Sept. 1, 1836, printed circular in the Wesleyan archives, Olin Library, Wesleyan University.

[25] Daniel Boorstin, *The Americans: The National Experience* (New York: Random House, 1965), pp. 152-161.

[26] George F. Pierce, "Church Colleges," an address delivered in Oxford, Georgia, February 22, 1852, on the occasion of the laying of the corner-stone of a new college building, in Atticus G. Haygood, ed., *Bishop Pierce's Sermons and Addresses* (Nashville: Southern Methodist Publishing House, 1886), p. 41.

[27] S. Olin to G. F. Pierce, Randolph-Macon College, December 7, 1835, in George G. Smith, *The Life and Times of George Foster Pierce* (Sparta, GA: Hancock Publishing Company, 1888), p. 79.

[28] Pierce, Church Colleges," p. 42.

[29] Donald G. Tewksbury, *The Founding of American Colleges and Universities Before the Civil War With Particular Reference to the Religious Influences Bearing Upon the College Movement* (New York: Bureau of Publications, Teachers College, Columbia University, 1932), p. 115.

[30] For a useful, though provocative, study of the topic of the development of personal and professional identity in nineteenth century America, see Burton J. Bledstein, *The Culture of Professionalism: The Middle Class and the Development of Higher Education in America* (New York: W.W. Norton & Company, 1976).

[31] *Methodist Magazine*, July, 1839, p. 272, cited in T. Michael Elliott, et al., *To Give the Key of Knowledge: United Methodists and Education, 1784-1976* (Nashville: National Commission on United Methodist Higher Education, United Methodist Church, 1976), p. 15.

[32] Bishop Matthew Simpson cited in David Sherman, *History of the Wesleyan Academy at Wilbraham, Massachusetts* (Boston: The McDonald & Gill Company, 1893), p. 6.

[33] Olin, *Life and Letters*, Vol. II, p. 86.

[34] Becker, p. 208.

[35] James McLachlan, "The American College in the Nineteenth Century: Toward a Reappraisal," *Teachers College Record* 80:2 (December, 1978): 294.

[36] *Journal of the General Conference*, 1820, p. 208.

[37] Markle, pp. 45-46.

[38] "Notes of Mrs. Fisk," p. 16.

[39] Ibid.

[40] Olin, *Life and Letters*, Vol. I, pp. 49-50.

[41] James Bryce, *The American Commonwealth* 2 vols., 3rd ed. rev. (New York: Macmillan and Co., 1895), Vol. 2, p. 626.

[42] Journal of the General Conference, 1832, pp. 399, 412-413.

[43] Minutes of the Indiana Conference, 1832-1844, published as Part II, William Warren Sweet, *Circuit-Rider Days in Indiana* (Indianapolis: W.K. Stewart & Co., 1916), pp. 101-103; cited in William Warren Sweet, *Indiana Asbury-DePauw University, 1837-1937* (Cincinnati: The Abington Press, 1937), p. 26.

[44] Peter Cartwright, cited in T. Scott Miyakawa, *Protestants and Pioneers: Individualism and Conformity on the American Frontier* (Chicago: The University of Chicago Press, 1964), p. 94.

[45] See for example, Sweet, *Indiana Asbury*, p. 27

[46] Miyakawa, p. 92.

[47] Donald G. Tewksbury, *The Founding of American Colleges and Universities Before the Civil War* (New York: Bureau of Publications, Teachers College, Columbia University, 1932), p. 104; Sweet, *Indiana Asbury*, p. 23-24.

[48] John Durbin, in *Quarterly Register*, August, 1831, p. 16; and *Methodist Magazine*, July, 1839, p. 272; cited in Tewksbury, pp. 108-109.

[49] Dwight Oliver Wendell Holmes, *The Evolution of the Negro College* (New York: Bureau of Publications, Teachers College, Columbia University, 1934), p. 141; Daniel A. Payne, *Recollections of Seventy Years* (New York: Arno Press, 1968), p. 225.

[50] Payne, p. 227.

[51] See Howard M. Kinlaw, "Richard Furman as a Leader in Baptist Higher Education, " (Ph.D. dissertation, George Peabody College for Teachers, 1960), pp. 54-64 for an overview of Furman's early educational work.

[52] Elmer Louis Kayser, *Luther Rice, Founder of Columbian College* (Washington, D.C.: The George Washington University, 1966), pp. 9-10.

[53] Kayser, *Luther Rice*, p. 15; David Bronson Potts, "Baptist Colleges in the Development of American Society, 1812-1861," (Ph.D. dissertation, Harvard University, 1967), p. 34; Elmer Louis Kayser, *Bricks without Straw: The Evolution of George Washington University* (New York: Appleton-Century-Crofts, 1966), pp. 38-39.

54 See Kinlaw, pp. 92-97; 111-119; 203-207; and Tewksbury, p. 115.

[55] Timothy L. Smith, "The Religious Foundations of Higher Education in Illinois," paper presented at the Shelby Cullom Davis Center Seminar, Princeton University, March 16, 1973, p. 1

[56] Smith, pp. 13-14.

[57] W.K. Woolery, *Bethany Years: The Story of Old Bethany From Her Founding Years Through a Century of Trial and Triumph* (Huntington, WV: Standard Printing & Publishing Company, 1941), p. 19.

[58] Robert Richardson, *Memoirs of Alexander Campbell* (Philadelphia: J.B. Lippincott & Co., 1870) II: 469-70, 591-91.

[59] Ben M. Barrus, Milton L. Baughn, Thomas H. Campbell, *A People Called Cumberland Presbyterians* (Memphis, TN: Frontier Press, 1972), pp. 194-95, 202.

[60] *Journal of the General Conference of the Methodist Episcopal Church, 1840* (New York: Carlton & Phillips, 1856), p. 163.

[61] See Richard Hofstadter, *Academic Freedom in the Age of the College* (New York: Columbia University Press, 1955, 1961), pp. 209-21.

[62] Sweet, *Indiana Asbury*, p. 48.

[63] Francis Wayland, *Thoughts on the Present Collegiate System in the United States* (Boston: Gould, Kendall & Lincoln, 1842), p. 35.

[64] Sweet, *Indiana Asbury*, p. 59.

[65] ibid.

Chapter VI
A REGULAR THEOLOGICAL TRAINING, AFTER THE SEMINARY PATTERN, WILL BREAK DOWN OUR ITINERANT SYSTEM

METHODIST OPPOSITION TO THE ESTABLISHMENT OF VANDERBILT UNIVERSITY

The March 2, 1872 issue of the *Nashville Christian Advocate*, the official journal of the Methodist Episcopal Church, South, carried a letter to the editor from one of the Bishops of that church, George F. Pierce. Bishop Pierce was angry, and he said so. Pierce was upset with the rapidly developing plans—reported regularly in the *Advocate*—to found a great "Central University" for his denomination, and to include in that university a fully developed theological seminary. He wanted to make it clear that on this subject, "the Bishops, I presume, are divided,"[1] and he was part of the opposition.

Pierce's letters were not directed to the Nashville journal by chance. For some time the editor of this journal had been part of a small group of intellectuals within the Methodist Episcopal Church, South, who had been agitating for a theological seminary for their "connection." And the *Advocate* had been one of the main vehicles for their publicity. The leader of this group was Bishop Holland N. McTyeire and it was logical that he should be the one to answer his fellow bishop in print.

For the next two months, from March to May, 1872, the two bishops carried on their debate in the pages of the *Advocate*, arguing their differing perspectives on the advantages and disadvantages of a graduate level theological seminary for the specialized, professional training of future ministers for the southern branch of Methodism. In this debate, as well as in an earlier debate at the General Conference of the Methodist Episcopal Church, South, which was held in 1870, and which was also well documented, the historian is offered an unusually clear picture of the thinking of both advocates and opponents of a major change in the direction of American education—the development of a post- college professional school for the training of Protestant clergy.

In subsequent versions of the Vanderbilt story, McTyeire usually emerges as the hero of the new institution while Pierce is dismissed, as he was by the author of his obituary in 1884, "His attitude towards education in the ministry was not of the advanced type."[2] More recent scholars have not seen fit to revise the opinion.[3]

The debate between these two bishops of the Methodist Episcopal Church, South must be seen as more, however, than a clash between an enlightened advocate of growth and a conservative who tried to hold back the tide. A more useful understanding of this conflict will be gained if it is seen as a debate between two differing understandings of the nature of Protestant ministry, and therefore only secondarily as a debate about the best institutional methods of preparing future ministers.

Seen in this light, Pierce must be viewed as a defender of a well established method of theological education, one which had been serving Methodists and allied denominations well for over half a century. It was not a method of education which did not value study. On the contrary, Pierce and his allies insisted on study by all ministers—study in the conference course and study in college when possible. They did not, however, believe that a college education was essential for the ministry, and they did not think that specialized graduate schooling for future ministers served the church well. The Methodist itineracy, with its ample opportunities for a long apprenticeship as a junior preacher rode the circuit with a senior one, was their preferred method of ministry and therefore of theological education.

At the same time, Bishop McTyeire and his allies were not, as Pierce sometimes charged, simply interested in importing a new method of schooling from the denominations which had founded Andover, Princeton, and other theological seminaries. They too were beginning with a concern for the nature of the ministry. And in this also they differed from Pierce. McTyeire made that point quite clearly. The Methodist ministry had changed. It was no longer primarily a ministry based on the itineracy—on large circuits—but on settled parishes. However much Pierce might dislike the change, McTyeire's argument began with his perception of the new reality that, "Railroads, and turnpikes, and telegraphs, and what not, have cut up the work. The people demand Sunday- preaching, and the pastor to live among them. The times, the age, lead to stations and small circuits."4 And if this was a reality, if Methodism was no longer a denomination of itinerant preachers but settled pastors, then like it or not, theological education had to change too. McTyeire accused Pierce of trying to hang onto a past that was gone—a past in the nature of the ministry first and only secondly in theological education. Thus McTyeire quoted an Methodist preacher who had begun his work in the 1820s:

The old plan of bringing in workers is gone; I saw it going out years ago. You can't fetch it back—no use trying. We must fall upon something that will do what the old plan did for us. I was once opposed to theological seminaries, and talked against preacher-factories as big as anybody, and I am opposed to them yet on the cast-iron plan of some folks; but we must have *something* to take the place of the old plan, and a theological school, guarded, and checked, and *Methodized*, is the best, and, to me, it seems the only substitute.5

Again and again, McTyeire and others made the same argument. They saw that the nature of the ministry had changed. And because of this change, there had to be a change in ministerial education. And like others before them they saw the best means of making that change the development of a new institution.

Because the arguments of both sides are so well recorded in the vigorous debates in the *Advocate*, as well as in the General Conference minutes and elsewhere, the struggle surrounding the first theological seminary within the Methodist Episcopal Church, South provides an excellent case study for examining the views of both winners and losers on the value of professional education in the nineteenth century American church, and also on the relationship of religion and larger cultural values.

In a very different context, the English historian E. P. Thompson has provided a helpful reminder that history need not merely be the story of the winners when he wrote:

> Our only criterion of judgment should not be whether or not a man's actions are justified in the light of subsequent evolution. After all, we are not at the end of social evolution ourselves.[6]

For historians of education, this should not be news. In the last generation historians such as Michael Katz have insisted that many of the successful causes and much educational reform has been "reform by imposition" and that the impositions have often failed to serve well the constituencies in whose benefit they were announced.[7] Both sides, those who fought to maintain the itineracy as a means of ministry and of theological education, and those who believed that a new style of ministry and therefore of theological education was needed, deserve attention if a clear picture of the changes taking place in both the nature of the ministry and of ministerial education in the years after the Civil War is to emerge.

The Anti-Seminary Position

George F. Pierce was an unusual person to lead the anti-seminary movement in its last stand. He was certainly not typical of the earlier generations of Methodist clergy, most of whom had received little or no schooling. On the contrary, Pierce was one of the first in his conference to be a college graduate. He had attended Franklin College in Athens, Georgia, graduating in 1829. And while there he had studied with the same Stephen Olin, who was soon to become one of the foremost advocates of college training for the Methodist clergy as

126

president of Randolph-Macon College and later Wesleyan University.[8]

In spite of his differences from the first generation of American Methodists, Pierce remained as clear as they that the heart and soul of Methodism was the responsibility of Methodist preachers to proclaim their own experience of conversion by the power of the Holy Spirit and call others to share in it. He wanted to make sure that the preachers had this sort of experience, and that they could share it in language understandable to their fellows.[9] The writer of his obituary recalled, "Bishop Pierce was never reckoned a close critical student: in learning he has often been surpassed. But....He was a genius in oratory....Bishop Pierce appeared to greatest advantage in the pulpit."[10] He wanted the same to be said of the next generation of Methodist preachers, and he believed Methodism already had a method of preparing them.

In his debates with McTyeire, Pierce described very clearly the positive form of theological education which he did want for Methodists.[11] He approved the requirement of a test for competence in the English language before admission to a conference on trial. More important, he supported the four year apprenticeship during which the candidate was expected to read through the course of study, while at the same time preaching—and feeling the pressure to improve his sermons. Pierce was confident that, "Conscience, the demands of the Church, the desire of acceptance and usefulness, fidelity to God, and the fear of disapproval at the Conference, all constrain him to study. He must improve."[12]

Pierce was defending both the structure of the Methodist ministry as it had emerged in North America in the first half of the nineteenth century, and the structure of ministerial education which was intimately linked with it. All ministers in this system were itinerant circuit riders who abandoned a settled life for the horseback ride through the wilderness with a charge to "preach in the morning, where he can get hearers."[13] Pierce saw himself as defending the complete system, both the method of ministry and the method of ministerial education.

One of Pierce's allies, J. W. Sassnett of Emory College warned Methodists not to "imitate the policy of other commun-

ions...."[14] After all, he asked, why should they? They already
had a better method of clergy training:

> The itineracy brings the preacher directly and at once into
> contact with practical life, and while it secures to him an in-
> creasing knowledge of men as they are found on the great
> theatre of action, it disciplines his powers and modes of
> popular adaptation to the actual wants of his hearers.
> Theological schools, on the other hand, establish a style of
> preaching and modes of thought without reference to the
> popular standard, and send out their preachers without
> adaptation to those upon whom they are designed to act.[15]

Sassnet was never opposed to education for the ministry. For
those who could take advantage of it, he strongly urged a
college education. And he wanted careful training to go on for
those already in the itineracy. In both places, skills could be
learned while one stayed in touch with a wide variety of people.
But he did not want "intermediate theological establishments in
which habits and tastes are acquired totally unfitting them for
practical efficiency."[16] Pierce agreed with this position. "Allow
me to say...," he wrote, "that a regular theological training, after
the seminary pattern, will complicate our itinerant system; will
slowly, but surely, modify it, and finally break it down."[17] Since
Methodism already had a uniquely successful means of both
ministry and ministerial training, he saw no need to tamper
with it.

In addition to what he considered a rugged apprenticeship,
Pierce made it clear that, like Sassnett, he supported colleges.
But he also insisted that the colleges be for everyone. Even the
work of the Biblical Professors in the colleges, Pierce insisted,
"should be open to all the students alike. There should be
nothing exclusive, technical, professional about it."[18] Still,
Pierce did believe college was desirable for a prospective
preacher.

> If an ignorant youth in his teens were to tell me he was
> called to preach, I would advise him to go to school; ay, I
> would send him to college, educate him as thoroughly as
> time and means allow....If a man who has reached his
> majority and over, and has been preaching as a traveling

preacher, were to come and ask me if I would advise him I would tell him no. I should urge him to study hard and preach on....[19]

College was useful, indeed important if the timing was right. But for Pierce, the focus also remained clear. The ultimate goal was saving souls, sharing an experience of the Holy Spirit. The test of all education was whether it aided that process or not. And for Pierce, the seminary certainly failed.

Prior to the Civil War, the vast majority of Methodists, north and south, shared Pierce's position. When the question of theological education was raised at the 1854 General Conference of the southern church, the Committee on Education voted that consideration of the issue was inappropriate.[20] Four years later the Committee reported "conflicting views" on the subject of ministerial education, but recommended only a tightening of the rules for the course of study and more opportunities to study the Bible in Methodist colleges.[21] All of these moves were quite consistent with Pierce's own position.

The Pro-Seminary Reformers

By the close of the 1858 conference, a small band of reformers, committed to the eventual development of a theological seminary in their denomination, had emerged, however. Their home was the publishing house in Nashville where Thomas O. Summers served as editor.[22] The two other most important members of the group were Landon C. Garland, President of the University of Mississippi and Holland N. McTyeire, who had just moved from a successful pastorate in New Orleans to join Summers at the publishing house in Nashville.[23] Eventually, McTyeire would be elected a bishop in his church and serve as President of the Board of Trust for Vanderbilt University, while Garland served as the school's first Chancellor and Summers as the first Dean of the Department of Theology. But there was more to endure before a university was founded than any of the reformers could have imagined in 1858. The quadrennial General Conference of 1862 never met. The Methodist Episcopal Church South almost ceased to exist as a connectional system.

Communication became impossible. The Civil War had intervened.[24]

Given the almost total disruption of southern life between 1861 and 1865, it is amazing that the reformers emerged so quickly from the conflict with both their ideas and their strategy intact. Indeed, when the General Conference finally met in 1866, their concerns were immediately included in the agenda. The Bishops' Address included the note that, "we specially bring to your attention the importance of an institute for the proper training of young preachers."[25]

The 1866 conference had yet more good news for the reformers. The Committee on Education—again without dissent—set two basic goals for ministerial education—the offering of a "full course" in theological education for those who would voluntarily use it and the setting of a "common standard of excellence" which would be required of all future preachers.[26] Of course, the committee was careful to note that there must be "no pretermission of the fundamental doctrine of a Divine call to the ministry and a spiritual preparation for it."[27] All Methodists insisted on that. But the development of minimum standards of intellectual competence did seem to challenge the traditional interpretation of the primacy of the Divine call. Finally, before adjourning, the conference elected McTyeire as a bishop, giving him a greatly expanded voice in future deliberations on the subject.

As they prepared for the next General Conference in 1870, the reformers clearly had every reason to be optimistic. Still, they developed their plans carefully and spread their ideas as widely as possible. In the fall of 1869 the *Advocate* carried a series of six articles on "An Educated Ministry" by Garland. In these he proposed that there should be a general raising of the educational standards for ministers, but there must also be "a theological institution of the first class, established by the authority of the General Conference—its chairs filled by the highest learning and the deepest piety of the Church—where our young men may be trained in all that appertains to an efficient discharge of the full work of a minister."[28]

Finally, at the 1870 conference itself, the Committee on Education, chaired this time by Garland, made its recommendation:

> We think the Church ought to establish a Theological
> Institute under the control of the College of Bishops, and
> officered by our wisest and holiest men, where those called of
> God to preach may receive without detriment to their piety
> and zeal a better preparation for the work of the ministry.[29]

The Institute would be required of no one, and no certain length
of stay would be necessary, although the school would offer as
one option a three year course to "meet the wants of the classical scholar...."[30] A minority of the education committee, however, offered an alternative:

> *Resolved.* That we endorse the action of the last General
> Conference in reference to Biblical Chairs in connection with
> our existing colleges, as the best available means of training
> young preachers.[31]

The Conference adopted the minority report. Apparently, the
majority of southern Methodists—or their delegates—still accepted the traditional distrust of theological seminaries, and
were not prepared to begin one.

Led by McTyeire, Garland and Summers, the seminary
proponents had no intention of waiting four more years for the
next General Conference to discuss the issue—and for their
opponents to organize. Acting through the Tennessee regional
conference, they arranged for a special convention of all interested regional conferences to meet in Memphis in January,
1872, to consider the founding of a University for southern
Methodism. Perhaps if the seminary were linked to the plan for
a new university, enough support could be garnered for the
school to start without General Conference approval.[32] To no
one's surprise, the Memphis convention agreed to the "establishment of a University of high grade"[33] provided an endowment
could be found. The new university was to have five departments, including undergraduate instruction and a theological
school.[34] It was then in response to the reports of the results of
the Memphis Convention, and the accompanying articles of
praise in the Nashville *Advocate*, that Bishop Pierce wrote his
own articles—reminding readers that not all Methodists were so
enthusiastic about the new school—and McTyeire answered

him. But public debate was not to settle the issue.

The controversy in the *Advocate* was short lived and came to an abrupt halt in the issue of May 18, 1872 with a notice from Bishops Pierce and McTyeire that:

> The controversy between us, growing out of the proposed Central University, comes to an end, with satisfaction to ourselves, and, we trust, without any damage to the Church, whose welfare we both have been seeking to promote. The occasion of it has been adjusted by the unanimous agreement of the College of Bishops, and upon terms agreeable to all the parties.[35]

The same issue also contained a more detailed report of the agreement which had been reached within the College of Bishops in their meeting of May 9, 1872. The Bishops had agreed to the request from the Central University Board that they choose the location of the new university—thus giving it a kind of episcopal sanction. But in return, McTyeire had made three important concessions to Pierce's position. First, nothing would happen until $500,000 had been raised. This was also required by the school's proposed charter, and this alone made any action highly unlikely in the post bellum south. Secondly, the Central University was to be seen as simply another college supported by regional conferences, exactly the same relationship to the church which all of the other colleges of the Methodist Episcopal Church South held. And exactly the same sort of relationship to the church which Pierce had been calling for all along and which McTyeire and others had been opposing. Finally, the Bishops agreed to view the Theological Department as merely the expansion of the Biblical Chair of the new university, and therefore exactly in line with the actions of the two previous General Conferences. This was the opposite of what the school's founders had been saying they were doing for the previous two years, but it got them the episcopal approval they so badly needed. On the rhetorical front, it looked like a victory for Pierce. But it was a victory on that front only.[36]

The strongest hurdle for the new school—the half million dollar requirement—was made without knowledge of McTyeire's relationship to a most unlikely financial resource, Cornelius

Vanderbilt. The men's wives were cousins, and the two got along well.[37] Less than a year after the Bishop's action, McTyeire could write happily to his wife, "The good news, hinted at before, will have reached you before this comes to hand."[38] Vanderbilt had given the $500,000, and would increase it to a million before he died.[39]

Avoiding the rest of the Bishop's agreement would be even easier. Since the school was a regional conference school, its own trustees and not the General Conference would set policy. McTyeire was elected President of the Board, and the rest of the plan unfolded smoothly. All that was left for the General Conference of 1874 to do was vote their thanks to the old commodore.[40] The following year, the new university opened its doors to students, including full-time theological students, and McTyeire took up his residence in the house on campus which Vanderbilt had provided for the President of the Board, to make sure that the supervision of the institution was well in hand. In spite of a variety of difficulties in the decades ahead, specialized, professional theological instruction had arrived in the Methodist Episcopal Church, South to stay. Pierce and his allies had lost the war.

Once he was defeated on the Vanderbilt issue, Pierce tended to drop the controversy. His views were not changed, but he would not fight an existing Methodist institution.[41] Still, more than hints of his old position came out. At the ordination of a group of deacons in 1879, seven years after the controversy, he warned these new ministers, "In these days, when the rage for education is so active and universal, I think our young preachers are in danger of adopting false views and wrong methods on the pretext of better preparation for their work."[42] "We must teach sound doctrine—must sow the wheat of God's truth, not the chaff of human inventions...."[43] It would not have taken his audience a lot of imagination to guess that he most likely still believed that an institution like Vanderbilt was more likely to produce "the chaff of human inventions," than serve as a source for "God's truth."

The Methodist Episcopal Church, South was one of the last major white Protestant denominations to found a theological seminary. Beginning with the work of Congregationalists at Andover, Massachusetts in 1808 and Presbyterians at Princeton, New Jersey in 1812, the three-year, post-college theological seminary quickly spread among American Protestants as the preferred, if not always the possible, means of training clergy. For this model to have been opposed as vigorously as it was when it was proposed among southern Methodists more than a half-century later is, in itself, an indication that important issues were at stake. An examination of these issues sheds light on the intellectual development of John Wesley's descendants in North America, and on the changing nature of the relationship of religion to the surrounding culture in the post-Civil War era. In at least three areas, the two sides were articulating different, but equally consistent, visions of Methodism and its ministry.

Office vs. Profession

Describing the changes in the mostly Congregational ministry in New England between 1750 and 1850, Donald M. Scott coined the phrase, "from office to profession."[44] While both the context and the meaning of the terms differ significantly in the post-Civil War south, his study still provides a useful model for the two differing images of the minister being debated among southern Methodists. For the reformers, the ministry was a profession, and deserved the best possible professional training. But it was exactly at this point that their opponents disagreed. For Pierce and his allies it was essential to remember that the ministry was not a profession at all, but an office to which one was called by God, and in which one did not exercise skills but witnessed to experiences. Unfortunately, for his cause, such a description of the ministry did not fit well with some of the most powerful trends in late nineteenth century America.

Burton J. Bledstein has well captured the emerging professional image when he wrote:

Hence, the culture of professionalism required amateurs to "trust" in the integrity of trained persons, to respect the moral authority of those whose claim to power lay in the sphere of the sacred and the charismatic. Professionals controlled the magic circle of scientific knowledge which only the few, specialized by training and indoctrination, were privileged to enter, but which all in the name of nature's universality were obligated to appreciate.[45]

It was this sort of moral authority which Landon Garland wanted for ministers when he wrote that a theological seminary was important because through it, "The social position of such a minister would be greatly elevated."[46] For Garland, this social elevation was important if ministers were to continue to receive respect in an increasingly professionalized society.

There were many in antebellum America who believed that "success in the middle class increasingly depended upon providing a service based on a skill, elevating the status of one's occupation by referring to it as a profession."[47] As E. Brooks Holifield has argued—

The term "professional" was more suggestive than precise in clerical comments, but clearly at its center was one ideal: the personal embodiment of knowledge....Professionalism was not so much the refinement of technical skills as the mastry of a body of knowledge, whether scientific, legal or theological, and of the foundational principles implicit in the application of the knowledge.[48]

The seminary, reformers such as Garland were persuaded, was the ideal means of accomplishing this "personal embodiment of knowledge." They struggled hard for the institution because they were convinced that with its establishment, future southern Methodist ministers would have the important advantages deriving from "high mental culture and from an extensive and varied store of knowledge. [And] Nothing gives more respectability to character or more weight to opinion; and these are the principal grounds of influence."[49] In their own eyes, these reformers were elevating the ministry and giving it influence which was essential if the message of their denomination were to continue to be heard.

From the perspective of their opponents, however, the reformers were not elevating but reducing the status of the ministry. Ministers like Pierce rejected the professional identity for the minister in favor of a much older description of the ministry—an office to which one was called by God. In a time when many Americans were rushing to adopt the new identity, Pierce and others stood with a minority in opposition.

Pierce was quite explicit in his position. "Let God call, the Church endorse, the Conference receive, and the Bishop send forth—urging them to read, study, pray, preach, work, and let these men be faithful, and they will be an honor to their race, and a blessing to the world."[50] All of the steps were essential for Pierce, but so was the order. The call of God had to come first. This was what gave the minister authority—not any special knowledge gained through training. If the sequence remained clear, if the ministry remained an office to which one was called first, then Pierce supported all of the study and training which a candidate could acquire. But he greatly feared that the order would become reversed, that candidates would be sent off to schools, cut off from the living experience of the "evangelist and the revival," and if that were allowed the only result would be that the preachers would be "spoiled by artificial, arbitrary, stereotyped 'training'."[51]

Because of his insistence that Methodism not be cut off "from sympathy with the mass and multitude of mankind by a scholastic isolation of her ministry,"[52] Pierce might be seen as a democratic opponent of a clerical elite. But this is a misleading picture. True he believed that Methodism had a mission to "the masses of society"[53] but he also believed that this mission was to be carried out by a very special elite, those called by God to the work. Ironically, he defended clerical privilege even more than McTyeire, opposing lay delegates at the General Conferences while McTyeire favored them.[54] Pierce's view of the ministry was high indeed, but it was a status based on values fading in importance by the last quarter of the nineteenth century.

Even after the end of the Vanderbilt controversy, Pierce continued to argue for his own understanding of the base of the minister's authority. Preaching to a group of new ministers he reminded them:

Many of us, brethren, will never write commentaries or
preach big sermons, but we can tell our experience, when we
were awakened; what we thought, felt, and feared; our
doubts, struggles, and temptations; and by the time we
reach the point where God converted us, if our own tears will
let us see, we shall find the audience weeping too.[55]

This sense of authority, based on one's ability to testify to one's
own experience of the Holy—calling the minister first to conversion and then to preaching—was something Pierce was quite
clear he would not trade for all of the professional authority
which an academic institution could confer. Unfortunately for
his cause, too few of his contemporaries agreed.

Different Understandings of Wesleyan History

As one reads the debates between those who supported and
those who opposed a theological seminary for southern
Methodism, it becomes clear that the two parties had quite
different readings of their own heritage. When the pro-seminary
reformers discussed Methodist history they looked to the English experience. John Wesley was remembered for his experiences at Oxford and for his role in the founding of Methodist
schools. For this group the current success of English Methodists in founding schools for training preachers represented an
extension of that same history; one to be emulated. The seminary opponents remembered Methodist history quite differently.
After a quick nod in Wesley's direction, they turned to the
American experience, beginning with the missionary work of
Francis Asbury and the frontier circuit riders for their models of
true Methodism. The English experience after Wesley's death
held no authority for those Americans.

Examples of the differences abound in the debates. At the
General Conference of 1870, Landon Garland began the report
of the Committee on Education with an historical reminder:

The assertion that Methodism is unfriendly to learning, or
that, at any time, it has disdained to avail itself of its advantages, is a libel upon a Church which was originated within
the walls of one of the most venerable and reknowned
universities of the world—a Church whose founder was a
man of extensive, and varied, and accurate knowledge, and

who, to the end of his life, did all in his power to improve the intellectual as well as the spiritual *status* of his followers.[56]

Garland's Wesley was the one who had once angrily responded to the charge that Methodists were required to renounce their reason by writing, "It is a fundamental principle with us that to renounce reason is to renounce religion, that religion and reason go hand in hand, and that all irrational religion is false religion."[57] With such roots, the future was also clear for Garland. Methodism in the postbellum south would also gain its "spiritual status" from the theological training offered to its leaders.

The same historical references continued into the debates of 1872. In one of his first articles supporting the moves toward the Central University, Holland McTyeire wrote in the Nashville *Christian Advocate* that he hoped it would help the planning for the University with its Theological school if his fellow Methodists knew more of the "origin and plan of theological education among the British Methodists."[58] He then traced their story from the founding of the Kingswood School by John Wesley in 1739 through the nineteenth century theological institutions serving British Methodists. If Methodism's founder was himself a university graduate and a founder of schools, it seemed logical to his heirs in the American south that they too should have a university which offered, among other things, the best possible theological training.

Their opponents, however, read Methodist history quite differently. At the debate at the 1870 Conference on the question of a theological seminary, the seminary opponents pointed to different origins for the Methodism they were defending. "Contrast our Church with other Churches," one delegate argued.

> Our Church has produced some of the greatest men of this or any other age, without theological training, or any other college besides God's great Word. Our Bascom drank his inspiration from the music of the spheres and learned his eloquence amid the high mountains and roaring cataracts of Kentucky's blue hills....[Munsey] was never in college or theological institution in his life, but all his inspiration and

138

power is found in his faith and power with God. Raised in East Tennessee, without any advantages, he has drank in his inspiration and power amid the great works of God—and he is today without a rival in our own or any other Church in Christendom.[59]

From Oxford University to Kentucky's blue ridge and the hills of East Tennessee was quite a move. Yet for the seminary opponents, the latter represented the real breeding ground of authentic Methodism. They were quite prepared to "contrast our Church with the Weslyan in England,"[60] and had no fears which would emerge with greater signs of God's blessing.

Writing in the Nashville *Christian Advocate* in 1872, another seminary opponent, Leroy H. Cage, reviewed his own experience and that of other frontier preachers, and urged, "keep up our old system; it has excelled all others, and try to improve in education, temporal and spiritual, and let the ministers try themselves to be learned."[61] For Cage, and many others like him, self-education, while engaged in ministry allowed much more room for the work of the Holy Spirit which institutions, he feared, could too easily shut out.

Pierce agreed with this focus on the success of Methodism in the American context. He wrote dramatically of the apprenticeship of the early frontier preachers in America, including his own experience with only "the Bible and the Discipline in my hands." And he was convinced that this was the best method of theological education. "Out of this old plan, with all its hard work, and with few books, mingling all the while with the uncultivated, came the men who shook heaven, earth, and hell."[62]

While it is obvious in this debate that each side was reading history quite selectively, it is a mistake to view the debate only in terms of Wesley and the English experience vs. Asbury and the American experience. The pro-seminary advocates did cite Wesley much more often than their opponents, but Pierce and his allies were also echoing an equally important part of Wesley's own understanding of the relationship of faith and reason.

For Bishop Pierce, the heart and soul of Methodism was the responsibility of Methodist preachers to proclaim their own experience of conversion by the power of the Holy Spirit and call others to share it. In a sermon, Pierce elaborated this position:

> Methodism was born when the world was piled full of other churches, filled to the rafters with dead forms and shadows of religious experience. Methodism came and brought to the world a live experience.[63]

He wanted to be sure that the next generation of Methodist preachers had this sort of "live experience," and that they could share it in a language understandable to their followers. And the real danger, for him, in a theological seminary, was that it could too easily substitute academic study for this basic experience.

In this focus on experience as the primary element in a religious tradition, Pierce was closer to the heart of Wesley's thought than his opponents. He was echoing the Wesley who wrote in his diary on the morning before his own conversion experience at Aldersgate that, religions experience was central to faith and that "none could have such faith without feeling it."[64] Wesley also elaborated this same position when he wrote:

> And until you have these internal senses, till the eyes of your understanding are opened, you can have no apprehension of divine things, no idea of them at all. Nor consequently, till then, can you either judge truly or reason justly concerning them, seeing your reason has no grounds whereon to stand, no material to work upon.[65]

Here in Wesley's words, if he had thought to quote them, was the heart of Pierce's argument. The seminary, Pierce feared, might raise the reasoning ability of the clergy—something he would support—but it could also too easily be a reason with, "no grounds whereon to stand, no material to work upon." Only the experience of conversion provided this material, and there was nothing in the plan for the new school which guaranteed this sort of experience. Indeed, Pierce feared a form of training which would leave a student "shut up in a seminary, lectured and molded by a given pattern, till all individuality is destroyed..."[66] He liked a more active means of education.

During the General Conference debates of 1870, one delegate argued against a seminary on the grounds that, "Methodism...desires and uses all light and learning, but can only make them effective when they blaze and burn with the Holy Ghost."[67]

Throughout the argument there remained the persistent fear that seminaries worked to stamp out the presence of the Holy Spirit. It seemed to these observers that the denominations who had adopted this innovation were producing preachers who had lost the spirit's power and become formal, but worse than formal heretical; refining the details of a faith which they no longer believed.

This was a very different reading of the Wesleyan heritage than Garland's or McTyeire's. It led Pierce to view their proposed seminary as an institution which could too easily turn his denomination to "dead forms and shadows of religious experience." No wonder he wrote, "I cannot 'conscientiously help forward the work' of providing a Theological School, and *therefore* I 'feel obliged to hinder it,' if I can fairly."[68]

Sect vs. American Denomination

Those who supported and those who opposed theological seminaries in the Methodist Episcopal Church, South differed in their description of the nature of the ministry, and in their vision of the historical roots of southern Methodism. They also differed in their vision of the future. And at that point, their differences mirrored some of the most profound choices faced by widely differing groups of Americans—to what degree did they want to be integrated into the general culture and to what degree did they want to maintain their uniqueness? In this debate, even more than in the other two, the historian must "read between the lines," for both sides were reluctant to state the issue directly, if they even recognized it. Yet, with some care, the issue emerges quite clearly.

For those who supported seminaries, the institution was one means among many for moving Methodism into the mainstream of American religious life. They compared themselves regularly with other denominations and found southern Methodism wanting. Bishop McTyeire expressed this fear of being left out quite well when he wrote:

A commission has been organized for revising our English Bible—a work in which all Protestant Churches are interested, and ought to be represented. British Methodism has two or three men on that commission; Northern Methodism one, and considering their strength, as compared with the denominations about them who have Andover and Princeton, and other old theological schools, they ought to have more. In each case these Methodists have supplied their representatives *from their theological schools*. Southern Methodism has no representative in that commission. Perhaps the old prejudice against the slave-region had something to do with this. But suppose we should complain, standing on the platform Bishop Pierce offers us? The commissioners could reply—"Gentlemen, you have some eloquent preachers and fervent evangelists—men who are a power among the common people—but *critics* are wanted for this work—scholars deeply learned in Bible lore—and by your own confession you don't produce the article. Confine yourselves to your mission among the masses, and take such a book as we make up for you."[69]

For McTyeire, the respect of other denominations was essential if his own was to take its rightful place in the spectrum of American Christianity. Numbers were valuable, but status was also essential.

Pierce had no use for such arguments. He had no use for a new translation of the Bible anyway. But the issue went far deeper. Pierce would not apologize for Methodism's unique role, but rather was proud of it. "Methodism does not occupy 'an inferior place', she never did," he argued, and "If she will stick to her own ways, and quit aping and imitation, she never will."

I, too, "claim for Methodism a mission to all classes." But I do not mean to cut her off from sympathy with the mass and multitude of mankind by a scholastic isolation of her ministry....The preaching that is fixed up, for the "cultivated and refined" is very poor preaching.[70]

In part, this was a class struggle. Pierce did see his focus for Methodism as the great majority of the [white] masses. The elite, he seemed to argue, could take care of themselves. He had little patience with McTyeire's desire for respect in other quarters.

Again and again, those who supported seminaries, argued

that the status of the ministry had to be raised or many of the best people would leave the denomination for others which offered more sophisticated preaching. As early as 1858, some were arguing for more schooling because of, "the wide-spread demand amongst all of our churches for a higher degree of intellectual cultivation in those who minister at their altars than was made in the earlier years of our history."[71] This theme continued throughout the debate. In the middle of the Pierce-McTyeire debate another writer noted in the *Advocate* that, "We cannot afford to let our sister Churches outstrip us on educational grounds."[72]

For Pierce, however, those who argued this way were missing the point. He had no fear of his form of Methodism being outstripped on educational grounds, for the issue, to him, was good education versus bad. And he knew which side represented each. He was happy to engage in comparisons with other denominations. "The Presbyterian training is too slow and stiff to meet the urgent and diversified calls of a promiscuous population," he insisted.[73] In the next article he continued the comparisons. "The Episcopal Church would have been nearly extinct by this time if they had not borrowed or beguiled ministers from us and others—mainly from us. Two-thirds of their clergy are recruits from other Churches. This old effete machine cannot turn them out fast enough even for the slow, stately progress of 'the Church.'"[74]

The debate was not one about facts. Both sides agreed that Methodism was one of the largest denominations and would continue to be so. But it was one of focus. McTyeire, Garland, and their allies worried about the cases of, "The sons of our most intelligent members, and in many cases, ministers, [who] are not satisfied with the facilities which we, as a Church, offer them; and, as a matter of fact, are seeking this culture in schools outside of our Church."[75] Pierce responded, if culture was their highest priority, let them go. Methodism had more important things to worry about.

> The Methodists and the Baptists have a ministry right out from the people—understanding their thoughts, feelings, and language; and however despised and berated, they are the

instruments which God has honored for the evangelization of the people.[76]

The essential focus of the debate, was whether Methodism would continue to keep this popular direction uppermost, or whether in an attempt to integrate itself with other denominations, it would shift focus. Seen in that light the stakes were considerably higher than whether or not one new educational institution was needed in Nashville.

By the time the battles over the founding of Vanderbilt were fought in the 1870's, those like Pierce who opposed the school were swimming against the tide. Too many forces within American society and even their own Methodist church were against them. They wanted to hold onto a vision of their tradition which was unique and powerful. But already, Methodism had lost much of what made it unique in the early years of the nineteenth century. Unlike some of his allies, Pierce did not want to merely hold onto the earlier ways of church life. Still, he did argue that "a regular theological training, after the seminary pattern, will complicate our itinerant system; will slowly, but surely, modify it, and finally break it down."[77]

The reality was, however, that well before the Civil War, the itinerant Methodist system had already begun to break down. Significant numbers of the clergy were no longer really itinerants but preachers "assigned to stations," that is, pastors of specific local churches. Others held a variety of other positions, teachers in academies and colleges, officers of benevolent societies, editors of religious journals. In Hunter Farish's felicitous term, the circuit rider had dismounted.[78] While important numbers of Methodist clergy would remain on their circuits throughout the nineteen century, the directions for the future were well set by the time of Pierce's battles.

Given this reality, McTyeire made his most telling point when he argued that apprenticeship, linked with a course of study, might once have worked well, but would no longer.

> The awkward, timid, ignorant young preacher was worked in harmony with an old seasoned, tried one. The old preacher encouraged him, taught him....[But now] The times, the age, lead to stations and small circuits. The list of appointments

in a large Conference may not have half a dozen preachers in couples: what used to be the rule is now the exception. Young men, raw, untried, at their first appearance, are sent to circuits and stations as preachers in charge....Sometimes the preacher breaks down under it; but oftener the congregation.[79]

The move from primarily rural and small town circuits to settled stations, very much like the pastorates of other denominations, had been going on for a long time.[80] Something new was needed, and the advocates of seminary training had the distinct advantage of knowing exactly what they believed would fill the bill.

Nevertheless, those who opposed these developments have deserved more historical attention that they have received to date. In his opposition to the institution which would be Vanderbilt University, George Pierce gave voice to those who defended an earlier form of Methodism—and especially the Methodist ministry. He was correct, more correct than his opponents dared admit or probably realized, that with the acceptance of specialized theological training, coupled with the already rapid development of stations or parishes in place of the older itineracy, an important phase of Methodist history had passed from the scene.

Methodism was becoming more and more like its sister denominations. Those who had seen in Methodism a unique and powerful version of the Christian church and who had witnessed its virtual sweep of a continent in the first half of the nineteenth century, had also seen a model of ministry and of theological education emerge and pass from the scene in their lifetimes. It deserved a better tribute than the next generation would allow it.

Conclusion

The battle over the founding of Vanderbilt was the last major battle within the larger white Protestant denominations in the United States regarding the establishment of theological seminaries. By 1875 every one of the larger denominations was operating a seminary of its own. While it would be another seventy-five years before the majority of clergy were actually graduates of these institutions, the theological seminary which was born at Andover in 1808 and Princeton in 1812 had in less than a century become the preferred means of schooling preachers. This had happened because those who favored the institution had been able to argue successfully that this means of education served better than any other to enhance the understanding of the ministry which was growing ever more popular throughout Protestantism in the years after the Civil War—the minister as a well trained professional. Those who sided with Bishop Pierce in active opposition to the institution—and to viewing the minister as a professional—would continue to be a smaller and smaller minority.

For the theological seminary, to emerge as the prefered means of ministerial education took the dedicated work of a generation of reformers in each of the denominations. Holland McTyeire and Landon Garland were late in a long line. Among northern Methodists, La Roy Sunderland, a young Methodist preacher, provoked a storm of protest in 1834 when he proposed in the *Methodist Magazine and Quarterly Review* that the New England Methodist conference establish a three-year theological seminary.[81] No doubt Congregationalist Andover, founded in 1808, Presbyterian Princeton, founded in 1812, and Baptist Newton, founded in 1825, provided the model for ministerial education which he believed Methodists should adopt.

The following issue of the journal carried a response calling Sunderland's seminary "a dangerous and ruinous innovation" and an idea which was "radically erroneous, and calculated to sap the foundations of the ecclesiastical structure"[82] In 1872 Sunderland recalled the debate:

> Now is it scarcely possible, for any one at the present time, to realize how very deep, and bitter the prejudice was, in the church against this movement, even so late as thirty years ago. By many it was supposed that to advocate scientific attainments in the ministry, was a sure evidence of a want of faith in God: and, any one "moved by the Holy Ghost to preach the gospel" had no need, whatever, of any literary qualifications for that work, and to advocate the establish-

ment of Theological Seminaries, it was thought, could only be done by a "backslider," or one who never had "the love of God shed abroad in his heart."[83]

What Sunderland failed to recognize was that those who were opposing him were not opposed to "any literary qualifications for the work," but had a different understanding from his of both the nature of the work of ministry and of proper preparation for it.

Those who joined in Sunderland's cause were helped by the reality that in northern Methodism even earlier than in southern, the circuit system had begun to break down. In urban areas Methodists were moving into the middle class and forming parish churches. The old methods of ministry and ministerial education were no longer adequate. And as the ministry changed, ministerial education had to follow.

In northern Methodism as in southern, the pro-seminary group succeeded by calling on the friendly conferences and ignoring the more hostile ones. Not surprisingly, the strongest support for a seminary was in New England—far from the heartland of Methodism, but close to the earliest Congregationalist and Baptist seminaries. When representatives from all of New England's annual conferences met in 1839, they decided to found a seminary. By 1843 the Newbury [Vermont] Biblical Institute had two full-time faculty members and twenty students. The Institute moved to Concord, New Hampshire, in 1847 and to Boston in 1868 where it became Boston University School of Theology.[84]

In the early 1850s, John Dempster—often referred to in Methodist literature as "the father of Methodist theological seminaries"[85]—decided that a second seminary was needed and moved west to found one. He was fortunate to make contact with a wealthy Chicago widow, Eliza Garrett, who agreed to a $300,000 bequest to found Garrett Biblical Institute. Dempster had discovered the most promising solution to the problem of support in a denomination largely ambivalent about his cause. Through outside benefactors a small group of educators was able to develop a series of institutions independent of the church, although they were quickly made accountable to it.[86]

147

Thus those who sought to change the Methodist understanding of ministry used the institutions of theological education as a first step towards their goal.

Dempster's success went beyond administrative skills and success at fund-raising. Perhaps more important was his ability to articulate a vision of the seminary as a means of strengthening rather than sapping Methodist identity. In a lifetime of sermons and pamphlets Dempster argued that the ministry did need special training, and that without it Methodists would quickly lose ground to other denominations. In one sermon in 1846 he argued:

> This elevated standard of ministerial attainment is demanded by the state of the times. The age is one of spreading intelligence,—of a widely diffused spirit of independent thinking....nor can we enjoy the requisite piety—without profoundly studying the Divine Word.[87]

Dempster's ally, Stephen Vail also argued that ministers needed this kind of instruction "before entering fully upon the discharge of their sacred functions."[88] Apprenticeship would no longer do, especially when the apprentice was physically isolated from the instructor—in a different parish, not sharing the same circuit.

Of course, there is nothing obviously different between the rhetoric Dempster used for seminaries and that used by Wilber Fisk or Stephen Olin in favor of Methodist colleges only a decade earlier. What was different was Dempster's success in linking these arguments with a particular institution, the post-college, three year theological seminary which had been such an anathema to Methodists of Fisk's and Olin's generation.

A similar pattern took place among Baptists. Richard Furman played a crucial role in the development of the first Baptist Conventions—seeing them as a means of support for both missionary work and theological education.[89] In May, 1817, Furman convinced the Baptist Convention meeting in Philadelphia to adopt a resolution in support of a "Theological Seminary and Library, under the care of learned, pious professors; in which theology shall be studied in its various branches."[90] Shortly thereafter such an institution was begun in Philadelphia, moved briefly to Washington, D.C. and then in

1825 to Newton, Massachusetts.[91]

After the Baptist Triennial Convention split in 1844 over the issue of slavery, the Southern Baptist Convention began plans for a central southern institution for theological education.[92] The Southern Baptist Theological Seminary was opened at Greenville, South Carolina in 1859, and although the disruption of the Civil War and the fact that the schools entire endowment was invested in Confederate bonds, meant that the school had to begin again after 1865, the pattern was set.[93]

This growing uniformity in the years after 1875 is all the more striking, because the early part of the nineteenth century saw such a profusion of new and different means of clergy training. When eighteenth century Presbyterians decided that they needed an institution to train the clergy for their faction in the divided Presbyterian church, they knew the model to which they wanted to turn—the college, whether at Princeton or Philadelphia. Early in the nineteenth century, when Trinitarian Congregationalists lost control of Harvard, they first considered founding a college of their own, but then developed a new institution, the post-college school at Andover. Elsewhere a wide variety of new institutions were born. The Methodists, Disciples of Christ, Cumberland Presbyterians, and the vast majority of Baptists had broken away from the long traditional insistence upon the ideal of a thorough classical education prior to ordination. While ministers might be educated along with the laity at colonial Harvard, there was only one route to the ministry—through college. In response to new understandings of the nature of the ministry which emerged in the nineteenth century, a new pattern of ministerial training developed. The seminary fit easily with the understanding of the ministry as it emerged among Presbyterians and Congregationalists, but as has been seen, it directly contradicted one of the fundamental commitments regarding the ministry among Methodists, as well as some Baptists and some of those who left the Presbyterian church.

It would be well into the twentieth century before Baptists and Methodists began to expect a seminary degree as a precondition for ordination. After 1875, however, no one seriously challenged the theological seminary's right to exist within most

Protestant denominations. While hostility greeted the founders of Vanderbilt in the 1870s as it had those who proposed a New England Methodist seminary in the 1830s, those prefering alternate modes of theological education came to recognize the seminary as one acceptable mode. Whether it was abolitionists in Oberlin, Ohio in the 1830s or unreconstructed successionists in Tennessee in the late 1860s, those seeking to provide a point of focus for their theological commitments chose the same institutional structure. In succeeding years the seminary would only grow in favor. The variety of methods of schooling preachers which had characterized the eighteenth and nineteenth centuries was not destined to continue.

FOOTNOTES

¹ G. F. Pierce, "Letter From Bishop Pierce," *Nashville Christian Advocate*, March 2, 1872, p. 14.

² "Bishop George F. Pierce," (obituary), *The Quarterly Review of the Methodist Episcopal Church, South* VI:4 (October, 1884): 591.

³ See Gerald O. McCulloh, *Ministerial Education in the American Methodist Movement* (Nashville: United Methodist Board of Higher Education and Ministry, 1980); Hunter Dickinson Farish, *The Circuit Rider Dismounts: A Social History of Southern Methodism, 1865-1900* (Richmond, VA: The Dietz Press, 1938); Charles T. Thrift, Jr., "The History of Theological Education in the Methodist Episcopal Church, South, 1845-1915," (M.A. thesis, Duke University, Durham, NC, 1932). All three authors do offer a useful overview of the founding of Vanderbilt.

⁴ Holland N. McTyeire, "Remarks on Bishop Pierce's Third Letter," Nashville *Christian Advocate*, May 4, 1872, p. 4.

⁵ ibid.

⁶ E.P. Thompson, *The History of the English Working Class* (New York, 1963), p. 13.

⁷ Michael B. Katz, *The Irony of Early School Reform: Educational Innovation in Mid-Nineteenth Century Massachusetts* (Boston: Beacon Press, 1968), pp. 19ff.

⁸ George G. Smith, *The Life and Times of George Foster Pierce, D.D., LL.D.* (Sparta, GA: Hancock Publishing Company, 1888), pp. 44-47; see also, Paul N. Garber, "George Foster Pierce," Dictionary of American Biography (New York: Charles Scribner's Sons, 1934), XIV: 580-581.

⁹ See George F. Pierce, "Character and Work of a Gospel Minister," (A discourse delivered before the ordination of deacons at the Holston Conference of the Methodist Episcopal Church, South, in Abingdon, VA., Sunday morning, Oct. 26, 1879) in Atticus G. Haygood, ed., Bishop Pierce's Sermons and Addresses (Nashville: Southern Methodist Publishing House, 1886), pp. 353-366.

¹⁰ "Bishop George F. Pierce," (obituary), The Quarterly Review of the Methodist Episcopal Church, South IV:4 (October, 1884): 586.

¹¹ Pierce, "Letter," *NCA*, May 18, 1872, p. 5.

¹² ibid.

¹³ The Doctrines and Disciplines of the Methodist Episcopal Church, 17th edition, (New York: D. Hitt & T. Ware, 1814), p. 34.

151

[14] J. W. Sassnett, "The Pulpit," *The Quarterly Review of the Methodist Episcopal Church, South* IV:4 (October, 1852): 565.

[15] ibid, p. 564

[16] ibid, p. 565.

[17] Pierce, "Letter," *NCA*, March 2, 1872, p. 14.

[18] Pierce, "Letter," *NCA*, May 18, 1872, p. 5.

[19] ibid.

[20] *Journal of the General Conference of the Methodist Episcopal Church, South,* 1854, p. 312.

[21] *Journal of the General Conference*, 1858, p. 550-552.

[22] E. Brooks Holifield, *The Gentlemen Theologians: American Theology in Southern Culture, 1795-1860* (Durham, NC: Duke University Press, 1978), p. 42.

[23] "Chronological Table," typed ms. in the Holland Nimmons McTyeire papers, Vanderbilt University archives, Nashville, Tennessee.

[24] For a detailed account of the experience of the Methodist Episcopal Church, South during the Civil War, see Farish, pp. 22-61.

[25] *Journal of the General Conference*, 1866, p. 20.

[26] Ibid., p. 135.

[27] Ibid.

[28] L.C. Garland, "An Educated Ministry—No. 6," Nashville *Christian Advocate*, November 13, 1869, p. 1.

[29] *Journal of the General Conference*, 1870, p. 236.

[30] Ibid.

[31] Ibid., p. 243.

[32] Thrift, pp. 51-58.

[33] W.L.C. Hunnicutt, "Central University," *NCA*, March 9, 1872, p. 10.

[34] Ibid.

[35] "A Note from Bishops Pierce and McTyeire," *NCA*, May 18, 1872, p. 9.

[36] "The Central University" (including a report of the actions of the College of Bishops of May 9, 1872), *NCA*, May 18, 1872, p. 9.

[37] Bard Thompson, "Vanderbilt Divinity School: A History," (Nashville: Vanderbilt University, 1958), 3; Farish, pp. 274-275.

[38] H.N. McTyeire to Dear A-, Monday, Mar. 17, 1873, handwritten correspondence, McTyeire papers, Vanderbilt University Archives.

[39] B. Thompson, p. 4.

[40] *Journal of the General Conference*, 1874, p. 577.

[41] Smith, p. 563.

[42] Pierce, "Character and Work of a Gospel Minister," p. 563.

[43] Ibid.

[44] Donald M. Scott, *From Office to Profession: The New England Ministry, 1750-1850* (Philadelphia: University of Pennsylvania Press, 1978).

[45] Burton J. Bledstein, *The Curse of Professionalism: The Middle Class and the Development of Higher Education in America* (New York: W.W. Norton, 1976), p. 90.

[46] L.C. Garland, "An Educated Ministry—No. 4," *NCA*, Oct. 30, 1869, p. 1.

[47] Bledstein, p. 34.

[48] Holifield, p. 34.

[49] L.C. Garland, "An Educated Ministry—No. 4," *NCA*, Oct.30, 1869, p.1.

[50] Pierce, "Letter," *NCA*, April 27, 1872, p. 14.

[51] Ibid.

[52] Ibid.

[53] Pierce, "Letter," *NCA*, March 23, 1872, p. 12.

[54] Garber, p. 581.

[55] Pierce, "Character and Work of a Gospel Minister," p. 361.

[56] "Report of the Committee on Education—No. 1," in "Proceedings of the General Conference of the Methodist Episcopal Church, South," *NCA*, May 18, 1870, pp. 1-2. (The *Advocate* reported the debate in more detail than the *Journal of the General Conference*.)

[57] John Wesley, *The Letters of the Rev. John Wesley, A.M.*, ed. by John Telford, 8 vols. (London: Epworth Press, 1931): Vol. V, p. 364.

[58] Bishop McTyeire, "Origin and Plan of Theological Education Among the British Methodists," *NCA*, January 6, 1872, p. 9.

[59] "Proceedings of the General Conference of the Methodist Episcopal Church, South," *NCA*, June 4, 1870, pp. 1-2.

[60] Ibid.

[61] Leroy H. Cage, "The Projected University," *NCA*, March 23, 1872, p. 14.

[62] Pierce, "Letter," *NCA*, May 18, 1872, p. 5.

[63] George G. Pierce, "The Distinctive Doctrine of Methodism," handwritten ms. of a sermon, n.d. (but post-Civil War), p. 6, George Foster Pierce papers, Georgia Department of Archives & History, Atlanta, Georgia.

[64] John Wesley, Journal of John Wesley; Vol. 1, p. 471-472.

[65] John Wesley, *The Appeals to Men of Reason and Religion and Certain Related Open Letters*, ed. Gerald R. Cragg, pp. 56-57, Vol. II of *The Oxford Edition of the Works of John Wesley*, gen. ed. Frank Baker (Oxford: Clarendon Press, 1975); for an excellent discussion of the relationship of religious experience and faith in the ideas of John Wesley, see Rex D. Matthews, "Reason, Faith and Experience in the Thought of John Wesley," unpublished paper, ©July, 1982.

[66] Pierce, "Letter," *NCA*, March 23, 1872, p. 12.

[67] *Journal of the General Conference*, 1870, p. 242.

[68] Pierce, "Letter," *NCA*, April 27, 1872, p. 14.

[69] McTyeire, "Remarks," *NCA*, April 6, 1872, p. 4.

[70] Pierce, "Letter," *NCA*, April 27, 1872, p. 14.

[71] "Report Number One of the Committee on Education," *Journal of the General Conference*, 1858, p. 550.

[72] "A Lady," "Bishop Pierce and the University," *NCA*, March 16, 1872, p. 15.

[73] Pierce, "Letter," *NCA*, April 27, 1872, p. 14.

[74] Pierce, "Letter," *NCA*, May 18, 1872, p. 5.

[75] D.C. Kelley, "Central University," *NCA*, May 18, 1872, p. 5.

[76] Pierce, "Letter," *NCA*, April 27, 1872, p. 14.

[77] Pierce, "Letter," *NCA*, March 2, 1872, p. 14.

[78] Farish, *The Circuit Rider Dismounts*.

[79] McTyeire, "Remarks," *NCA*, May 4, 1872, p. 4.

[80] See Holifield, pp.16-17.

[81] La Roy Sunderland, "Essay on a Theological Education," *The Methodist Magazine and Quarterly Review*, 16, (October, 1834): 426.

[82] David Meredith Reese, "Brief Structures on the Rev. Mr. Sunderland's 'Essay on Theological Education,'" *The Methodist Magazine and Quarterly Review* 37 (January, 1835): 117.

[83] La Roy Sunderland, handwritten manuscript, April 22, 1872, p. 4, in the New England Methodist Historical Society files, Boston University School of Theology, Boston, Massachusetts.

[84] For an account of these early years see, Eleanor Rust Collier, "Origins of Boston University School of Theology," typewritten ms., Boston University School of Theology Archives, Boston, Massachusetts.

[85] ibid, p. 14.

[86] See *Semi-Centennial Celebration: Garrett Biblican Institute* (Evanston: n.p., 1906).

[87] John Dempster, "The Study of the Scriptures," *The American Pulpit* 2 (June, 1846): 31-33.

[88] Stephen M. Vail, *Ministerial Education in the Methodist Episcopal Church* (Boston, 1853), p. 158.

[89] While often overstated, Furman's influence in the development of Baptist theological education, north and south, cannot be denied. Harvey T. Cook, *Education in South Carolina Under Baptist Control* (Greenville, South Carolina: n.p., 1912), pp. 34-35 describes Furman's role most positively. Howard M. Kinlaw, "Richard Furman as a Leader in Baptist Higher Education," (Ph.D. dissertation, George Peabody College for Teachers, 1960), p. 54, while uncritical, gives a more balanced view.

[90] "Proposed Resolutions, including a scheme of Education, having for its object the assistance of pious young men designed for the gospel ministry, which were laid before the Baptist Convention at Philadelphia, in May, 1817," quoted in its entirety in Kinlaw, pp. 199-201.

[91] See A. H. Newman, *A History of the Baptist Churches in the United States* (New York: The Christian Literature Co., 1894), pp. 398-400; Elmer Louis

Kayser, *Bricks without Straw: The Evolution of George Washington University* (New York: Appleton-Century- Crofts, 1966), pp. 38-51; Alvah Hovey, *Historical Address Delivered at the Fiftieth Anniversary of the Newton Theological Institution, June 8, 1875* (Boston: Wright & Potter, State Printers, 1875).

[92] Kinlaw, p. 145.

[93] William Wright Barnes, *The Southern Baptist Convention, 1845-1954* (Nashville: Broadman Press, 1954), pp. 129-133; John A. Broadus, *Memoir of James Pettigru Boyce* (New York: A. C. Armstrong & Son, 1893), pp. 119-121; Archibald T. Robertson, *Life and Letters of John Albert Broadus* (Philadelphia: American Baptist Publication Society, 1901), p. 144.

INDEX

157

JAMES W. FRASER is a member of the faculty of the College of Public and Community Service and a Senior Associate of the John W. McCormack Institute of Public Affairs at the University of Massachusetts at Boston. He is also currently Special Assistant to the Chancellor at the Massachusetts Board of Regents of Higher Education. He received his B.A. from the University of California, Santa Barbara, his M. Div. from Union Theological Seminary, New York, and his Ph.D. from Columbia University. In addition to this study, he is the author of *Pedagogue for God's Kingdom: Lyman Beecher and the Second Great Awakening* (University Press of America, 1985). He has also written for various journals on the history of Protestant theological education in the United States, and on the history and public policy issues in public education, serving as co-editor of *From Common School to Magnet School: Selected Essays in the History of Boston's Schools*. He is currently at work on a history of the Boston schools during the progressive era. In addition to teaching and writing, Dr. Fraser is pastor of Grace Church, Federated in East Boston, Massachusetts.